TRANSACTIONS OF THE
AMERICAN PHILOSOPHICAL SOCIETY
HELD AT PHILADELPHIA
FOR PROMOTING USEFUL KNOWLEDGE

VOLUME 69, PART 3 · 1979

The Foundations of English Bankruptcy:
Statutes and Commissions in the Early Modern Period

W. J. JONES
PROFESSOR OF HISTORY, UNIVERSITY OF ALBERTA

THE AMERICAN PHILOSOPHICAL SOCIETY
INDEPENDENCE SQUARE: PHILADELPHIA
July 1979

Library of Congress Catalog
Card Number 78-73169
International Standard Book Number 0-87169-693-2
US ISSN 0065-9746

PREFACE

Bankruptcy has been a hobby of mine for twenty years, a topic looked at casually when time allowed but often interrupted when considered seriously. Across so many years my debts to individuals and institutions have been many. One of the greatest is to the Huntington Library and its staff. Indeed the first version was put together in 1962 when, with the aid of a Huntington grant, I was working on Chancery and Ellesmere. Much is also owed to subsequent assistance from the Canada Council and the Guggenheim Foundation. This is for G.B.J.

ABBREVIATIONS

Adam Smith: Smith, A. S. *The Wealth of Nations,* ed. E. Cannan (New York, 1937).

Additional: Additional manuscripts, British Library, London.

APC: Acts of the Privy Council of England.

Atk.: Atkyns' Reports [26 *English Reports*].

BIHR: Bulletin of the Institute of Historical Research.

Blackstone: Blackstone, W. *Commentaries on the Laws of England,* ed. E. Christian (4 v., London, 1809).

Brown. & Golds.: Brownlow and Goldesborough's Reports [123 *English Reports*].

Bulstrode: Bulstrode's Reports [80 *English Reports*].

Chan. Cases: Cases in Chancery [22 *English Reports*].

Coke, *Fourth Institute:* Coke, E. *The Fourth Part of the Institutes of the Lawes of England* (London, 1669).

Co. Rep.: Coke's Reports [76-77 *English Reports*].

Commons Debates 1621: Commons Debates 1621, ed. W. Notestein, F. H. Relf, and H. Simpson (7 v., New Haven, 1935).

CJ: Journals of the House of Commons.

Cro. Car.: Croke's Reports, temp. Charles I [79 *English Reports*].

Cro. Eliz.: Croke's Reports, temp. Elizabeth I [78 *English Reports*].

Cro. Jac.: Croke's Reports, temp. James I [79 *English Reports*].

CSP Dom.: Calendar of State Papers, Domestic.

CSP For.: Calendar of State Papers, Foreign.

D.K.Rep.: Report[s] of the Deputy Keeper of the Public Records.

Ec.HR: The Economic History Review.

EHR: The English Historical Review.

El.: Bridgewater and Ellesmere manuscripts, Huntington Library.

Eq. Ca. Abr.: Equity Cases Abridged [21-22 *English Reports*].

Goodinge: Goodinge, T. *The Law Against Bankrupts: Or a Treatise Wherein the Statutes Against Bankrupts are Explained* (3rd ed., London, 1713).

Harleian: Harleian manuscripts, British Library, London.

H.M.C. Hatfield: Historical Manuscripts Commission, Manuscripts of the Marquess of Salisbury.

History: History (The Journal of the Historical Association).

Holdsworth: Holdsworth, W. S. *A History of English Law.*

Hutton: Hutton's Reports [123 *English Reports*].

Keble: Keble's Reports [83-84 *English Reports*].

Lansdowne: Lansdowne manuscripts, British Library, London.

LQR: Law Quarterly Review.

L. and P. Henry VIII: Calendar of Letters and Papers, Foreign and Domestic, Henry VIII.

LJ: Journals of the House of Lords.

Ld Ray.: Lord Raymond's Reports [91-92 *English Reports*].

Mod.: Modern Reports [86-88 *English Reports*].

Monro: Monro, C. *Acta Cancellaria* (London, 1847).

Nottingham's Cases: Nottingham's Chancery Cases, ed. D. E. C. Yale, Selden Soc. (2v., 1954, 1961-1962).

Nottingham's "Manual" and *Nottingham's "Prolegomena": Lord Nottingham's "Manual of Chancery Practice" and "Prolegomena of Chancery and Equity,"* ed. D. E. C. Yale (Cambridge, 1965).

Noy: Noy's Reports [74 *English Reports*].

Plucknett: Plucknett, T. F. T. *A Concise History of the Common Law* (5th ed., London, 1956).

P.R.O.: Public Record Office, London:
- C.24: Chancery Town Depositions.
- C.33: Chancery Entry Books of Orders and Decrees.
- C.38: Chancery Reports and Certificates.
- C.39: Chancery Supplementary Reports and Certificates.
- C.67: Chancery Patent Rolls, Supplementary.
- C.193/5: Chancery Miscellaneous, Crown Office Precedent Book.
- Durham 4: Palatinate of Durham, Entry Books of Orders and Decrees.
- E.215: Commission on Fees, James I and Charles I.
- E.333/17: Exchequer First Fruits and Tenths, Miscellaneous Book of Precedents.
- S.P.11: State Papers Domestic, Mary.
- S.P.12: State Papers Domestic, Elizabeth.
- S.P.14: State Papers Domestic, James I.
- S.P.39: Original Warrants for Grants.

Sanders: Sanders, G. W. *Orders of the High Court of Chancery* (London, 1845).

Tothill: Tothill's Chancery Reports [21 *English Reports*].

TRHS: Transactions of the Royal Historical Society.

Yelverton: Yelverton's Reports [80 *English Reports*].

THE FOUNDATIONS OF ENGLISH BANKRUPTCY: STATUTES AND COMMISSIONS IN THE EARLY MODERN PERIOD

W. J. Jones

CONTENTS

I. INTRODUCTION

The English law of bankruptcy is rooted in the assumptions and the legislation of Tudor and early Stuart society. It was then that the essential distinction between bankrupts and other debtors was made. In consequence most debtors, however great their liabilities, could not go bankrupt. During the formative hundred years of this story, debtors were many but bankrupts few. Furthermore, social distinctions may have been reflected even in the fate of those who could have gone bankrupt. Great merchants, although there are some celebrated examples, were an exception. Lesser merchants appear more frequently, but they were not a notable element. The majority of bankrupts were craftsmen, shopkeepers, and small middlemen: bakers and butchers, simple drapers and mercers, buttonsellers, fishmongers, and upholsterers. Between 1592 and 1596, the largest number of known bankruptcy commissions, approximately one-third, was sued out against chapmen.[1]

Before the Restoration, bankruptcies were infrequent. The annual average for the late Elizabethan and Jacobean periods may not have been much above ten, given that more commissions were probably granted in depression years. Between mid-September, 1630, and mid-March, 1631, an official reported transmitting payments for only four commissions issued with respect to persons living in the city of London and its vicinity.[2] In the disturbed years between 1642 and the king's execution in January, 1649, the annual average of enrolled commissions was about twenty-five, the thirty-eight granted in the twelve months from March, 1643, being an exceptional total. In 1652, sixty-eight commissions were awarded, but there were only thirty-one and forty-one in 1653 and 1654 respectively.[3]

It may be that the above figures are underestimates. The details are scattered, and for much of the period commissions were not enrolled. On the other hand, the evidence for 1642–1654 is fairly coherent. During these years, there was a separate series of rolls for bankruptcy commissions. Furthermore, the practices of Chancery clerks do not seem to have been unduly hindered by national events.[4] Nonetheless, it would still be unsafe to assume that all commissions were enrolled, although it is tantalizing to speculate that in this instance civil war might have been the background to greater competence than had been provided by former years of peace. However that may be, it is safe to conclude that bankruptcies, as distinct from failures, were not common, and that their number was in stark contrast to the amount of critical attention devoted to the subject.

In part, this was because the existence of the bankruptcy law had an impact which was much greater than that of its actual operation. It was something to be avoided, and hence the habits of businessmen were influenced. It is clear that many persons, often with the aid of established commercial customs, secured arrangements prior to total disaster, before they committed a technical act of bankruptcy, or even—when the creditors were compelled by mutual self-interest—after these events. If so, much contemporary criticism of the bankruptcy statutes can be modified, although it may not be dismissed. On the other hand, it seems very probable that bankruptcy was commonly avoided as much through calculation as caution. Before 1624, there are grounds for believing that legislation was a failure because the wording of statutes was often inadequate to sustain a claim from creditors that bankruptcy had occurred. This was one reason why con-

[1] The references are in El., scattered between 3043 and 5646.

[2] P.R.O., E.215/2/227.

[3] P.R.O., C.67/76a-85.

[4] For the general problem posed by patent rolls, see R. B. Pugh, "The Patent Rolls of the Interregnum," *BIHR* 23 (1950): pp. 178–181.

temporaries were so critical, and their observations may help to explain the apparent paucity of commissions granted.

Whatever the precise numbers may have been, the incidence of bankruptcy during the period under consideration is insignificant in comparison with the eighteenth century. Indeed the House of Commons, shortly after the Napoleonic Wars, was told that there had been over forty thousand bankruptcies since 1732.[5] Yet there is much to be learned from earlier years, not least because bankruptcy is one of those words which tends to be misused or have multiple meanings. This has bedevilled appreciation of the subject. How often have we heard of bankruptcy with respect to persons who were not, and who could not conceivably have become, bankrupts in law? Our understanding of other circumstances, technicalities, and terms is equally uncertain. The context of explanation is unsatisfactory, inevitably so, and we will only start to have a less than feeble grasp of early modern English society when more of its details have been studied.

Bankruptcy is one detail, a condition often mentioned but rarely understood, a label more likely to be employed with confidence than comprehension. There are dozens of such subjects awaiting exploration. Much has been written about social matters, from prosperity to poverty, without a basic understanding of the bonds, contracts and obligations, or their procedures and significance in law, which provide so much of the data. Bankruptcy as a theme is just one of many. Edward Jenks described it as important but uninteresting. Yet the topic is evocative, for this technicality born of statute was a hinge between law and commerce, a link welded in parliaments which were largely composed of men who dabbled much but belonged properly to neither world. An inquiry into bankruptcy, however limited the subject may seem, provides a poignant illustration of the way in which social distinction and economic fact were meshed with the formulation of law and the methods of its administration. Furthermore, business difficulties and collapses have not received the attention which they deserve.[6] This does not mean that a study of bankruptcy during the early modern period will shed much light upon the fortunes of those who traded. Despite adverse comment from some contemporaries, there is little reason to suppose that commerce was either harmed or helped.

The period between the first bankruptcy statute (1543) and the great civil war, virtually the Tawney Century, has been selected although the evidence is dispersed and nebulous. There is nothing to compare with the later wealth of detail to be found in law reports, treatises, business documents, and the official bankruptcy records of the eighteenth century. Certainly, a proper history of English bankruptcy from the Restoration can and needs to be written on the basis of conventional if complex sources. Before that time, the situation is different and the method has to be different. Some later material has been used, and general excursions attempted, but only in the sense that subsequent situations both reflect upon and were the product of earlier years.

A central feature of early bankruptcy arrangements was the appointment of commissions, a device which was crucial to Tudor notions of administration.

If economic fact and social assumption provided the bone and the flesh of Tudor and early Stuart society, the crown and the Council were the head. Institutions at Westminster, whether always present, like the Exchequer, or occasional, like Parliament, represented major organs of the system. Power, requirement, and responsibility flowed to various arteries: provincial councils, palatine authorities, shires, hundreds, and boroughs. The manor and other little units can be likened to the smaller vessels. Common to this structure was the way in which people were grouped in approved associations. As with guilds and companies, these might be essentially independent although authorized and approved by the state. Then there were commissions, notably those that were a direct creation of the state. A significant few were statutory, but many were institutional in their origin. Some were reasonably permanent, whereas others were temporary.

Recognition has always been accorded to the justices of assize and to some major commissions which were regularly renewed: for example, the High Commission and the provincial councils at Ludlow and York. The celebrated justice of the peace was a commissioner. Less attention has been paid to many short-lived commissions, statutory or otherwise, which operated at every level of English society. These were notable for their variety of membership and function. They might include eminent persons and lawyers, but lesser if nonetheless respectable citizens were of at least equal significance. Commissioners aided the assessment and collection of taxes, the settlement of disputes, and the administration of a multitude of practical problems. They supervised drainage, regulated grain exports, arbitrated disputes, examined witnesses, and surveyed boundaries. In the Elizabethan and early Stuart period, we can be sure that there were dozens, perhaps hundreds, of these and other commissions in existence on any given day. This was part of the reality of government on the grassroots level for a regime which

---

[5] *Suggestions Respecting the Improvement of the Bankrupt Laws* (London, ?1819), f. 2.

[6] See comments made by: R. S. Lopez and I. W. Raymond, *Medieval Trade in the Mediterranean World* (New York, 1955), p. 290, n. 1; V. P. Carossa, "The Waltham Watch Company: A Case History," *Bull. Business Hist. Soc.* (Dec., 1959): pp. 165–187. Some aspects are explored by R. A. Church, "Business History in Britain," *The Jour. European Econ. Hist.* 5 (1976): pp. 209–228.

claimed to exercise a sweeping responsibility although it did not have the sinews of a nation-wide bureaucracy. A sudden cessation of this activity would have endangered the fabric of order and possibly destroyed it. This shadow was apparent in 1640 and 1642.

Temporary commissions, such as those authorized by the early bankruptcy acts and the statutes of sewers, had as many differences and distinctions as were to be found in and between other organs of administration, great or small. Each type of commission was subject to particular instructions according to its task, but there might be broad variations between individual commissions which ostensibly handled similar problems. However, the demand for special skills and specific knowledge was a common factor, not least because the ability of businessmen and lawyers was so diverse. Two outstanding Chancery men, William Lambarde and John Tyndall, had reason on their side when they begged the bench to commission some merchants to help with the analysis of a disputed account concerning figs, since they themselves did "not thoroughly discern of the same." [7] Moreover, there was always need for familiarity with a locality and knowledge of particular persons. The membership of a successful commission was likely to balance many requirements.

Blackstone described the English law of bankruptcy and related Tudor innovations as "capital alterations of our legal polity" which were "highly convenient to that character, which the English now began to reassume, of a great commercial people." Adam Smith was less assured. Bankruptcy was "perhaps the greatest and most humiliating calamity which can befall an innocent man. The greater part of men, therefore, are sufficiently careful to avoid it. Some, indeed, do not avoid it; as some do not avoid the gallows." These two writers of the eighteenth century, a lawyer and a political economist, nonetheless agreed that bankruptcy had to be considered as a legal circumstance.[8]

A major problem for the historian is that the word *bankruptcy* has been used in two senses. The first is provided by general usage, literary or vernacular, covering people who have become destitute or insolvent, or in which we may, for example, speak of a king or a country as being "on the verge of bankruptcy." The general impression is one of financial calamity. The word is also used to support adverse comment on the intellectual, moral, or political standing of a government, institution, or person—"Bankrupt of life, yet prodigal of ease." [9] This range of meaning can be legitimate for many periods and countries: for Scotland, an authority has noted that "the word by itself has no place at all in the formal language of the law." [10] In England, on the other hand, the terms *bankrupt* and *bankruptcy* have represented a legal concept for over four centuries. This second understanding can be explained by reference to one definition of a bankrupt:

> One who has done some act or suffered some act to be done in consequence of which, under the laws of his country, he is liable to be proceeded against by his creditors for the seizure and distribution among them of his entire property.[11]

The crucial point is that of a man becoming "liable" under "the laws of his country," laws which in England were provided by statute.

One could wish that historians of post-medieval England would avoid using the words *bankrupt* and *bankruptcy* unless the legal meaning is intended. This hope is somewhat futile since contemporaries, including lawyers, used the words to indicate all shades of meaning. In 1571, a member of Parliament—possibly John Popham, a future speaker of the Commons and chief justice of the Queen's Bench—spoke of "treasurers of the Crown, who have in their hands great masses of money, with the which either they themselves or some friends of theirs do purchase lands to their own use, and after become bankrupt." He instanced a debt of £30,000 which had supposedly led to a shortage of money in the Exchequer. Bankruptcy legislation was being prepared at the time, and it is not impossible that he considered such behavior to warrant inclusion. There is insufficient evidence, and a separate act was passed making the property of receivers, tellers, and similar officials liable to payment of their debts.[12]

Statutes which created the law of bankruptcy were mundane attempts to establish new rules within the limited field of debt. They were commonplace and practical measures intended to provide solutions to a selection of immediate problems. These characteristics explain their most obvious defect, a failure to comprehend the complexity of existing law. Later legislation was hardly more successful, and in any case commercial conditions were constantly changing. Debt collection was not the only area where casual reform by statute resulted in fresh intricacies. Statutes poured forth with respect to charities and the criminal law, labor conditions, and imports. Legislation became more detailed as it became more frequent. "Parliament having once taken up a subject was apt to return to it

[7] P.R.O., C.38/3, pt 1, ff. 362b–363, Aldon and Humphrey v. Westwray (24 June, 1600).

[8] Blackstone **4**: p. 430. Adam Smith, p. 325.

[9] Note the examples of usage listed in *The Oxford English Dictionary*.

[10] A. D. Gibb, "Insolvency," *An Introduction to Scottish Legal History*, Stair Soc. **20** (Edinburgh, 1958): p. 222. Prior to 1696, "bankruptcy" and "insolvency" were used as synonymous terms in Scotland. H. Goudy, *A Treatise on the Law of Bankruptcy in Scotland* (Edinburgh, 1914), p. 15.

[11] *Teevan and Smith's Business Law*, by L. Y. Smith, G. C. Robertson, and R. A. Sprecher (St. Paul, 1951), p. 1129.

[12] J. E. Neale, *Elizabeth I and her Parliaments, 1559–1581* (London, 1953), pp. 219, 224.

again and again, piling act upon act, sometimes with confusing results."[13] In the nineteenth century Basil Montagu, an experienced bankruptcy commissioner, remarked that since its inception the bankruptcy law and its administration had been continually fluctuating and a subject of complaint. "As the existing statutes have been found to be insufficient to check existing frauds, or have themselves been productive of injustice; or as new frauds have presented themselves, new statutes have been enacted but the complaints yet continue."[14]

Social conditions may change, procedures and principles of law may develop or be adapted, but bankruptcy proceedings have always had some common objectives and weaknesses. A Stuart commentator on bankruptcy would not, I think, find much alien content in a 1975 report on this subject.[15]

Perhaps we expect too much, but Francis Bacon, for one, did think that the method of drawing up laws in his time was faulty. He was unhappy with the failure of preambles to outline the aims of legislation, and with the obscurity of words in the body of the statute which reflected back on the preamble.[16] The balance and clarity of language within statutes were increasingly important since the early modern period was marked by rapidly changing conditions which transformed authority, enforcement, precedent, procedure, and record. Above all, as Professor Thorne has noted, acts of Parliament had attained a new status by the middle of the sixteenth century. Emphasis would increasingly be placed upon their sanction and not merely upon their contents.[17] Lawyers, legislators, and litigants had an understandable difficulty in coming to terms with novelty. Yet even after according due recognition to these factors, the statutes can seem weak in their construction, expression, and meaning. As with the related areas of debt, imprisonment, and sequestration, it may be surmised that with respect to the evolution of English bankruptcy law generations of men succumbed to that old tendency by which the advantage of experience is squandered.

In a period of just over eighty years, from 1543 to 1624, there were four bankruptcy statutes.[18] There might have been further Stuart legislation but for the failure of Charles I's early parliaments and the troubles of the Long Parliament and Interregnum. Opportunities for statutory amendment were thus destroyed or dissipated. Hence, the task of clarification belonged increasingly to the judges. Faced by specific cases, they had to define the limits of bankruptcy jurisdiction and make adjustments of detail in accordance with the texts of statutes up to and including that of 1624. Whether or not this can be described as subordinate legislation is a moot point.[19] In general Stuart judges, even when faced by novel circumstances, kept close to the statutes. Bankruptcy remained firmly grounded upon legislative provision:

> Bankruptcy is entirely the creation of statute law. There is no such thing as a common law of bankruptcy, although the term is sometimes applied to certain rules of bankruptcy law not to be found specifically enacted in bankruptcy statutes but laid down from time to time by the judges exercising the bankruptcy jurisdiction.[20]

A principle of later bankruptcy proceedings—that "equality is equity"—was always present.[21] Early statutes were intended to secure the property and assets of the bankrupt and distribute them ratably between his creditors. Essential elements were sequestration of assets and the need to impose restraint upon those creditors who might seek full repayment at the expense of others. There was no intention of assisting the bankrupt. The initiative in suing out a commission had to come, at least ostensibly, from creditors. Provision was not made for a petition from the debtor and thus for voluntary bankruptcy. The bankrupt's discharge was introduced in 1705, but even in the twentieth century release from debts has been described as being never more than incidental to the law of bankruptcy.[22]

Early statutes assumed the bankrupt's delinquency. Their tone was condemnatory but this was not always of assistance to creditors, particularly those who under different circumstances might have been willing to grant further time for repayment or make other kinds of concession. Once a bankruptcy commission was sued out, the creditor's freedom of maneuver was circumscribed. Creditors had to swim with the tide or face the possibility of losing all that was due. Furthermore, the tendency to lump bankrupt debtors into a single category was questionable. Bankruptcy was nurtured as a technical and legal notion which only imperfectly fitted the realities of commerce, and yet it only applied to commercial men. Problems of capital,

[13] Plucknett, p. 325.

[14] B. Montagu, *Inquiries Respecting the Courts of Commissioners of Bankrupts and Lord Chancellor's Court* (London, 1825), p. 5.

[15] *Bankruptcy,* a report by "Justice," Allan Heyman, Q.C., chairman of committee (London, 1975).

[16] *The Works of Francis Bacon,* ed. J. Spedding, R. L. Ellis, and D. D. Heath (Boston, 1857–1874) **9**: pp. 322–324.

[17] S. E. Thorne, introd. to *A Discourse upon the Exposicion & Understandinge of Statutes* (San Marino, 1942), pp. 51, 54.

[18] 34 and 35 Henry VIII c. 4 (1543); 13 Elizabeth I c. 7 (1571); 1 James I c. 15 (1604); 21 James I c. 19 (1624). These four statutes will henceforth be referred to by date and clause. *The Statutes of the Realm* (11 v., London, 1810–1828).

[19] Plucknett, p. 335. A belief that such a power was being approached was one factor behind the attempted impeachment of judges in 1641, although bankruptcy was not then a matter of concern.

[20] Halsbury's *Laws of England* (London, ed. 1953) **2**: p. 251.

[21] W. H. Schrampeter, *Law in its Application to Business* (New York, 1941), p. 883.

[22] H. Remington, *A Treatise on the Bankruptcy Laws of the United States* (4th ed., Rochester, 1934) **1**: pp. 1–2.

investment and assets, credit and the availability of cash, were irrelevant. Hence Professor Supple has reason to conclude that for the Tudor-Stuart period bankruptcies are not "as good an index of crises in overseas trade as some historians have imagined." [23] After all, bankruptcy law was created by parliaments controlled by landed men and at a time when the legal profession was dominated by conservative influence and propertarian assumptions. "They continued to try to squeeze the fast multiplying problems and disputes of an adventurous commercial community into the antique legal framework devised for settling the problems of a small class of landowners." [24]

The Privy Council and the court of Chancery provided alleviation in a few cases, but these avenues of discretion, strenuously debated during the reign of James I, were limited by the 1624 statute. There are indications that the situation was again more flexible by the late 1630's. It is possible, but not proven, that during this critical period of Charles I's reign there was some official sympathy with those who might lend the crown money. On the other hand such persons, under normal circumstances, were not those most likely to be treated as bankrupts. Political considerations apart, there was always a sense that some distinction should be made between debtors whose inability was due to misfortune or chance, and those whose circumstances were the consequence of dishonesty, fraud, or reckless behavior. A law which concentrated upon the group rights of creditors was of little help to honest debtors, whereas it might be manipulated by dishonest ones.

With respect to both bankrupts and debtors, argument up to and including modern times has been reminiscent of the sixteenth-century controversy as to whether a line could be drawn between the willful and the unfortunate unemployed. There has been plenty of sympathetic comment, some of it even from the authorities, but bankruptcy as an evasion or as a stepping-stone to greater fortune attracts the public eye. As a lawyer said recently, there can be an impression that the bankrupt drives off in a Cadillac while his creditors trudge home in the snow. "Bankruptcy is when you put your money in your hip pocket and let your creditors take your coat." [25] Thomas Dekker, well before he himself endured over six years' imprisonment for debt (after 1612), made the necessary distinction between the unfortunate and the "politic" bankrupt, by which term he evidently embraced the type of man who managed to evade the bankruptcy statutes. The latter was a "harpy," a "hyena," a "mermaid," a "chameleon," or a "puritan." "It is not the honest bankrupt undone by suretyship, casualties or losses by sea, but a politic bankrupt, a noble-in-the-pound bankrupt, a five-shillings—nay, a ten-groats-in-the-pound bankrupt, a voluntary villain, a devouring locust, a destroying caterpillar, a golden thief." [26]

Debate had little impact, and it is not surprising that the law itself was seen by some as destructive. Were not the statutes as much a cause of bankruptcy as they were a remedy for some particular situations of debt? Doubts about bankruptcy combined easily with general criticism of the legal system aired with some strength after Naseby and Langport. Discontent was also apparent under the later Stuarts, by which time a clear distinction had been drawn between investment and active participation in trade. A real problem continued to be that those to whom the statutes applied, essentially tradesmen and merchants, had played only a minimal part in their construction. The situation was a far cry from the later Benthamite notion of good laws. It is not surprising that great merchants were sometimes critical of the statutes, but those most affected in practice, small tradesmen, had even less opportunity to be heard.

Describing acts of bankruptcy and establishing procedures to secure a ratable division of assets, the statutes created a quasi-jurisdiction. This was quite natural. Legislation in other areas invented or refurbished bodies which had varying degrees of relationship with, and independence from, established courts of law. The history of commissions required to handle charitable uses, marine insurance contracts, sewers, and other problems indicates that in each case a different tale unfolds. In every instance, nonetheless, the current state of law was a major factor. The early bankruptcy statutes created a type of commission which was thrown into the sea of courts and jurisdictions, limitations, procedures, and statutes which already existed. This was to be of the utmost importance not because the common law had all that much to offer but because it had done little to evolve provisions adequate for the circumstances of trade. Procedures for dealing with contract and debt were complex, and the English court system never really came to grips with that most popular of all Tudor and early Stuart devices, the recorded bond. Hence the 1543

[23] B. E. Supple, *Commercial Crisis and Change in England, 1600–1642* (Cambridge, 1959), p. 10. This is so despite the probability that some collapses were not, strictly speaking, bankruptcies. It is also worth noting the point that clothiers seem to have been more exposed in times of slump than were merchants. In more modern times, as the laws changed, there does seem to have been such a relationship. See R. C. O. Matthews, *A Study in Trade-Cycle History: Economic Fluctuations in Great Britain. 1833–1842* (Cambridge, 1954), pp. 16, 19.

[24] M. Birks, *Gentlemen of the Law* (London, 1960), p. 87.

[25] *Colombo's Canadian Quotations* (Edmonton, 1974), pp. 179–180.

[26] T. Dekker, *The Seuen Deadly Sinnes of London* (1606), in *The Non-Dramatic Works of Thomas Dekker*, ed. A. B. Grosart (New York, 1963) 2: pp. 17, 21; *Lanthorne and Candle-light* (1608), in *Thomas Dekker*, ed. E. D. Pendry (London, 1967), p. 275.

statute was so vague as to be nearly unworkable, and the 1571 statute was so restricted that it unbalanced the English law of bankruptcy for generations. The consequences can be seen in statutory amendments of the seventeenth century and in the limitations and interpretations offered by Westminster judges.

Under Henrician legislation, bankruptcy was handled by specified great officials, one of whom was the lord chancellor. The 1571 statute, in contrast, gave sole authority to the lord chancellor to issue commissions and to determine their composition. For a time there were two systems in existence, but the Henrician form of proceeding withered away. Eventually commissions under the Elizabethan statute, although issued individually, came to be surrounded by a permanent form of organization. The story is typical of that process whereby a remedy is taken up as a matter of government, translated into law, and eventually mechanized. Coke reflected this when he devoted a section of his *Fourth Institute* to "the court of the commissioners upon the statute of bankrupts." [27] This approach invites comparison with a description of nineteenth-century metropolitan bankruptcy commissioners as being "London's main commercial court." [28] It is, therefore, particularly important to be wary of diverse usages of the word *court*. It is true that the seventeenth-century creation of a Register for metropolitan commissions was important with respect to the beginnings of administrative cohesion. However, Elizabethan and Jacobean parliaments did not endow bankruptcy commissions with the attributes of a court. Procedures were crudely outlined, clerical requirements were ignored, and all the statutes were amorphous on the subject of ultimate administrative and legal responsibility.

Nonetheless, bankruptcy commissions did have a distinct identity. Furthermore, as Blackstone pointed out, none of the statutes allowed for appeal from the associated and personal jurisdiction exercised by the lord chancellor.[29] Yet in practice the decision of commissioners that a man was in fact a bankrupt, the prime point of importance for the debtor and his creditors, could be challenged at law. The statutes implied something about this, but not very much, and they appeared to hope that a state of bankruptcy could be assumed provided that it was sworn that a certain type of person had committed a certain type of action. It also came to be understood that the lord chancellor could not refuse a petition for issue of a commission, although Thomas Coventrye, lord keeper from 1625 to 1640, appears to have been ready to exercise discretion in some circumstances. Only in the mid-seventeenth century was the order of possibilities clarified: a debtor who denied bankruptcy could have his denial debated before a court of law, but the commission must first issue.[30]

Bankruptcy commissioners were not judges. Unlike justices of the peace sitting in Quarter Sessions, and distinctly unlike commissioners of sewers, they had only an authority and not a jurisdiction. They had to be wary of exceeding their powers. Experience advised care, and it is probable that sometimes this mitigated the intention of the statutes. There was no alternative, since the performance of bankruptcy commissions also depended on the law as expressed by other statutes or applied by a variety of courts.[31]

In the second half of the seventeenth century, some difficulties were resolved. This was largely due to interpretations offered by Lord Chancellor Nottingham. His work provided a clearer grasp of broad principles and helped to shape Chancery jurisdiction in the years between 1673 and 1682. Many aspects, nonetheless, remained unsatisfactory, not least because classification according to occupation remained a dominant factor. The discharge was introduced in the early eighteenth century, but other legislative experiments were less satisfactory. Complaint ranged from charges of inefficiency to doubts about the probity of those who operated the system. These were to be standard themes discussed well into the Victorian period. In introducing the bankruptcy act for Scotland (1856), the lord advocate remarked that pressure had been put on him to introduce the English law of bankruptcy, "which he had resisted on the ground that our own law, even unreformed, was better and less expensive." [32]

In the twentieth century, bankruptcy laws and procedures have been criticized for reasons which are historically familiar. Why, it has been asked in the United States, was there such a dramatic rise in the number of bankruptcies during the twenty years after 1945? Were not these years generally reflective of prosperity and rising incomes? A team of researchers concluded that the subject received little attention from scholars and the media unless spectacular individuals—business tycoons or film stars—were involved. They also questioned the very basis of bankruptcy arrangements. "Administratively, the bankruptcy system as it is managed through the courts violates most principles of sound organization and management. The system provides inadequate supervision, audit and investigation, leading to opportuni-

[27] Coke, *Fourth Institute*, p. 277.

[28] E. Welbourne, "Bankruptcy Before the Era of Victorian Reform," *The Cambridge Historical Journal* 4 (1932) : p. 51.

[29] Blackstone 3 : p. 427.

[30] See below, p. 27.

[31] This was still true of the nineteenth century. A warrant issued by a statutory commission might be considered as without authority, and a bankrupt who failed to answer questions "satisfactorily" could be released from prison on *habeas corpus*. A. Rubinstein, *Jurisdiction and Illegality* (Oxford, 1965), p. 111. See, 2 Chan. Cases, 72–73, Perrat v. Ballard (1681).

[32] Gibb, p. 227.

ties for error and fraud. Procedures are slow and archaic; records are incomplete and sloppy."[33] Similar conclusions have been reached, similar comments made, across four hundred years of Anglo-American history.

II. THE FIRST BANKRUPTCY STATUTE

Tudor statutes can be arid documents, but in recent years research has uncovered fascinating stories which help to explain Henry VIII's statute of appeals, the statutes of uses and wills, the "whipping" statute of 1547, the statutes which made up the Elizabethan church settlement, and the celebrated statute of artificers. This work supports Plucknett's suggestion that the apparent dryness of the statute book may be little more than a corollary of ignorance about the historical background. He pondered the contrast between the attitudes of historians and those of contemporaries for whom a statute might have a catastrophic character.

> It has the force of law on "the appointed day"; the day before that, all is void. How it came about is nobody's business; the recommendations (perhaps by an eminent body of commissioners) which initiated it, are irrelevant; the slow fashioning of it in debate and in committee, and the changes it underwent there, are no concern of the lawyers.[1]

In 1543, when the first bankruptcy statute was passed, the government and members of both houses were probably influenced most by the apparent ineptitude of existing rules applying to debt. Their major concern must have been with matters within common law jurisdiction. Maritime and mercantile practice, which in the Middle Ages had spawned a variety of local customs and codes, can have had little relevance to their deliberations. The law merchant, that is, the custom of the merchants, never matched the international strength of canon and civil law. Furthermore, merchant courts in England had not developed to the same degree as in some other places, although the mayors of the staples, usually but not always distinct from the borough mayors, had once enjoyed considerable independence and exercised a nearly exclusive jurisdiction over the persons and goods of merchants trading there.[2] C. T. Carr wrote about "our merchants' independence of the common law," but this does not mean that they could rely unduly upon the law merchant.[3]

Tudor and early Stuart men, whose law was essentially the law of the land, experienced tortuous difficulty in comprehending the technical requirements of commerce, both international and internal. One consequence was that methods of contract, credit, and investment hardly measured up to the requirements of business. Note can be taken, however, of the development of joint-stock companies and thus of a device geared to prospective profits. The bill of lading—in which a ship's master acknowledged receipt of specified goods and undertook to deliver them to a particular consignee—emerged to join the charter-party, a form of mutual contract between master and merchant. The development of the marine insurance contract did something to meet the uncertainties of overseas trade. These and attendant legal arrangements suggest a coming together of Tudor innovation and the "ancient" customs of the merchant community. Nor is it inappropriate to look forward to a gradual "incorporation" of the law merchant within the law of England, a process associated with a great series of judges culminating with Mansfield. However, this has very little to do with the development of English bankruptcy law. Holdsworth, by placing his principal treatment of this topic in a section on the law merchant, obscured discussion of the subject.[4] The bankruptcy statutes, far from having anything to do with the law merchant, were reappraisals of some points which lay within English law as it applied to chattels, debts, land, and sequestration.

It also has to be emphasized that although merchants, those who exported and imported, were embraced by the bankruptcy statutes, the key word was "trader." Middlemen, retailers and wholesalers, often small, made up the mass of businessmen. Their activities were rarely international or even national, and their status was remote from that of those who engaged in high finance. Yet the absence of this distinction is a curious feature of bankruptcy statutes insofar as they grouped together ordinary traders and common shopkeepers, minor manufacturers and great merchants. Indeed the statutes seem to display a blind disregard of the facts and habits of business life. Perhaps this was implicit in existing legal assumptions. "The common law," writes Harding, "was inclined to see commercial life as made up of masters and servants, of classes of person, each with its place and function in the social order, rather than in terms of individual enterprise and contracts."[5]

A mercantile approach towards bankruptcy may have matured in Europe with the collapse of some

[33] David T. Stanley, Marjorie Girth, and others, *Bankruptcy: Problem, Process, Reform* (Washington, D. C., 1971), pp. vii, 1–3.

[1] T. F. T. Plucknett, "Some Proposed Legislation of Henry VIII," *TRHS*, 4th ser. **19** (1936): p. 120.

[2] L. S. Sutherland, "The Law Merchant in England in the Seventeenth and Eighteenth Centuries," *TRHS*, 4th ser. **17** (1934): pp. 149–176. E. E. Rich, "The Mayors of the Staples," *The Cambridge Historical Journal* **4** (1933): pp. 120–142.

[3] C. T. Carr, *Select Charters of Trading Companies (1530–1707)*, Selden Soc. (1913), p. xiv. For a major attempt to sort some of the scanty evidence, see M. M. Postan, *Medieval Trade and Finance* (Cambridge, 1973), pp. 28–91.

[4] Holdsworth **8**: pp. 99–300 (especially pp. 229–245).

[5] A. Harding, *A Social History of English Law* (London, 1966), p. 310.

Italian companies which had been founded in the thirteenth and early fourteenth centuries on the basis of capital derived from interest-bearing loans.[6] Trade, even during the late medieval slump, had been substantial,[7] and at all times it was founded upon an intricate system of financial devices. The medieval period is rightly renowned for its condemnation of usury, but the doctrine of "just price" was flexible. The loaning of money implied a transfer of ownership and there was an obligation for this to be returned. The creditor or seller could justifiably be compensated for any damage, and it was not absurd to construe tardy repayment as a damage.[8] A number of maneuvers, notably those associated with the exchanges, could be employed to ensure a profit. Rates of interest were often quite high. There were, however, restrictions other than those provided by ethics. Although cash transactions must not be underrated, it has been suggested that inelasticity of credit was of major importance. "Medieval capitalism, precocious and adventurous as it was, was sporadic in its incidence. Its progress was hampered by forms of wealth difficult to negotiate. Markets were small, and the spirit which dominated them was local and exclusive." [9]

The great fairs were at the heart of emerging bankruptcy rules. It was presumed that creditors should receive at least part of the sums owing to them as easily and as quickly as possible. A general idea, stemming from Roman law, was that the property of the debtor should be divided equally among the creditors.[10] Under such localized circumstances and procedures, the danger was that emphasis upon the collective equality of creditors would result in disappointed men complaining that the debtor was being treated with undue favor. This discouraged those who might otherwise have drawn a distinction between deliberate and unfortunate debtors, and it aided in the development of fairly stringent rules. In many places, a merchant unable to meet his creditors could be imprisoned and his impounded property sold to satisfy debts. If the amount due was not covered, he might have to endure a further term in prison. He was also liable to expulsion from his guild or other commensurate loss of civic rights. The strict legal possibilities may have been harsher: debtors unable to meet their full obligations could be imprisoned in irons, and a "bankrupt" merchant was apparently beheaded at Barcelona in 1360.[11] Quite naturally, however, the main objective was an effective recovery of debts. This may have been related to the development of rules which encouraged the defaulter to seek resource in flight. Once the act of flight became a customary act of bankruptcy, it was convenient to develop procedures around this circumstance. Some creditors discovered that there were few remedies available when a debtor declined to run away and so had not committed an act of bankruptcy. Fiction sometimes provided the solution, it being supposed that "flight" had occurred.[12]

Flight, fictitious or real, provides a major theme, but it was not the only factor. "Anyone who fails to meet his engagements at the fair settling-days is held for bankrupt," wrote an early fourteenth-century Italian merchant about the Champagne fairs. "He completely loses his credit and cannot show his face." This system for assessing solvency had "the important defect that it acted both too seldom and too late." [13] After all, most creditors were interested either in satisfaction or some kind of composition. Hence, there was the advantage of establishing or presuming an act of flight before the settling day. Behavior which could be construed as an act of bankruptcy opened the way for procedures which gave a particular power to intermediaries. At the fairs of Champagne, it was understood from the twelfth century that a debtor's goods were to be construed as mortgaged to pay his debts. Preference was given to unpaid vendors, and creditors within the fair shared by rate. Creditors outside the fair were excluded from these arrangements, and they could only seek satisfaction from any assets that remained. A majority of creditors, in respect of the money owed and their numbers, could conclude an agreement or composition binding upon the minority. While the discussions went on, the defaulter might even be provided with a safe-conduct and protection against molestation. Provisions such as these, and they were of course marked by local variation, persuaded some people that things were being made too easy for debtors.[14]

[6] *The Cambridge Economic History of Europe,* ed. M. M. Postan and E. E. Rich (Cambridge, 1952) 2: p. 319.

[7] Although a slump existed, notably in the north and west of Europe, it should not be seen out of context. Medieval trade was significant in comparison with population, and later "trade expansion" had much to do with expanding population. The point is made by J. Bernard in *The Fontana Economic History of Europe: The Middle Ages,* ed. Carlo M. Cipolla (London, 1972), pp. 309–310.

[8] Iris Origo, *The Merchant of Prato* (London, 1963), p. 151.

[9] Violet Barbour, *Capitalism in Amsterdam in the 17th Century* (Ann Arbor, 1963), p. 11.

[10] Holdsworth **8**: p. 229. For a survey of international origins, see L. E. Levinthal, "The Early History of Bankruptcy Law," *University of Pennsylvania Lew Review* **66** (1918): pp. 223–250.

[11] Lopez and Raymond, p. 290. R. S. Smith, *The Spanish Guild Merchant: A History of the Consulado* (Durham, N.C., 1940), pp. 25, 27, 58.

[12] I. Treiman, "Escaping the Creditor in the Middle Ages," *LQR* **43**: p. 231.

[13] R. Ehrenburg, *Capitalism and Finance in the Age of the Renaissance* (London, 1928), p. 318.

[14] Lopez and Raymond, pp. 290–302. F. R. Sanborn, *Origins of the Early English Maritime and Commercial Law* (New York, 1930), p. 164. For further examples and the danger of hybrid solutions, see R. de Roover, *Money, Banking and Credit in Mediaeval Bruges* (Cambridge, Mass., 1948), pp. 332–336.

There are inherent pitfalls in assuming too much about "medieval rules" or in essaying generalizations about conditions "on the continent." Although some English developments were doubtless akin to those in Europe, the general impression is that they may have been inadequate for commerce and remarkably unfair to both creditors and debtors. "In all early systems of law," commented Holdsworth, "each creditor is left to pursue his own remedy." The creditor would be inclined to enforce his rights against the property in societies accustomed to organized commerce, credit, and industry. In medieval England, however, the debtor's obligation was of a highly personal nature in that his body could be taken by the creditor.[15] Building on this factor, the Tudors would fashion a statutory law of bankruptcy, a law promulgated by the state as distinct from one which was essentially a convenience to fairs and trading communities.

The statute of 1543 was specifically directed against debtors who fled or who kept to their houses. One theory is that debtors had previously used other means of evasion but that these had gradually been restricted.[16]

A degree of protection had been provided by the doctrine of sanctuary. Insofar as church or monastery was concerned, this had been restricted in the fifteenth century, notably by a papal bull of 1487 directed against dishonest debtors. Events of the 1530's confirmed this trend, but sanctuary remained a significant loophole during and after the Henrician Reformation. It had been most complete in a quarter of Westminster and in liberties such as St. Martin le Grand. An act of 1540 eliminated the old structure in favor of eight "cities of refuge," but many sanctuaries continued although they were questionable in law. Sanctuary as an escape from criminal process was now severely limited, but the testimony and experience of Defoe tell us that it continued to provide protection to debtors.[17]

Another means of escape had been restricted during the fifteenth century. When assets were hidden it had been possible for the creditor to obtain a judgment in an action of debt, and then to secure the imprisonment of the debtor on a *capias ad satisfaciendum* in order to aid execution of the judgment. Debtors had apparently been able to get themselves removed from custody if they could obtain a *corpus cum causa* from Chancery. In that court they could produce indentures and other evidences in defeasance of the original recognizances, so prompting a *scire facias* which required the creditor to appear in Chancery and answer the petition. Until this was done the debtor would be released on a bond, endorsed by a surety, which in default was payable only to the king. According to Treiman, the sureties were often discharged from this liability and so the creditor was left without resource. This device was probably of some use to debtors seeking to escape their obligations, but a statute of 1433 compelled sureties to bind themselves to both the creditors and the king.[18]

The real weakness was not the debtor's ability to evade execution, and sometimes custody, pending execution, but the inadequacy of execution itself. The ability of creditors to seize the assets of a debtor was seriously limited. A sheriff empowered by *fieri facias* could only seize property which he could sell, although from the late thirteenth century half of the debtor's freeholds, under some circumstances, could be taken in execution of a judgment for debt or damages.[19] This was not good enough, and in any case the creditor's position was restricted by defenses which surrounded the debtor. Until the nineteenth century, for example, it was impossible in execution of a judgment to seize choses in action—bills of exchange, checks, banknotes, and bonds. Then there was the relationship between personal immunity and personal property. This often meant that jewelry or clothes which were worn, or any personal property clutched in the hand or carried, might not be capable of seizure.[20] However, the person was not immune, and so imprisonment of the debtor remained fundamental to execution.

Imprisonment tended to be either custodial, as when punishment was the purpose, or coercive, for example when the aim was to enforce collection of debts. Both intentions applied when a person was confined for impeding or disobeying the process or decision of a court.[21]

Imprisonment of crown debtors was an established practice, but the application of such coercion against private debtors has its own story. Acton Burnell (1283) and the statute of merchants (1285) permitted imprisonment under certain conditions, but it was the statute of 1352 which ranked the common creditor with the crown insofar as it allowed imprisonment of the debtor's body until satisfaction had been obtained. "From this statute sprang all the imprisonings for debt, all the debtors' wards, and all the lamentations which they brought in their train." If the Fleet was initially the most famous home of debtors, other

[15] Holdsworth **8**: p. 229.

[16] Treiman, pp. 230–237.

[17] *Ibid.*, pp. 235–236. Plucknett, p. 431. 32 Henry VIII c. 12. Sanctuary was one of the actions mentioned by the Elizabethan statute. 1571, *1. D. Defoe, *An Essay Upon Projects, 1697* (Menston, 1969), pp. 223, 225. See Isobel D. Thornley, "Sanctuary in Medieval London," *Journal of the British Archæological Society*, new ser. **38** (1932–1933): pp. 293–315. I am grateful to Mr. W. Kellaway for this reference.

[18] Holdsworth **8**: p. 231. Treiman, p. 235. 11 Henry VI c. 10.

[19] 13 Edward I c. 18.

[20] G. P. Costigan, Jr., "Those Protective Trusts which are Miscalled 'Spendthrift Trusts' Reexamined," *Legal Essays in Tribute to Orrin Kip McMurray*, ed. M. Radin and A. M. Kidd (Berkeley, 1935), pp. 89–90.

[21] See R. B. Pugh, *Imprisonment in Medieval England* (Cambridge, 1968).

prisons were not far behind. Ludgate was closed for a time in 1419, apparently because too many private debtors preferred to lodge there in preference to meeting their obligations.[22]

Imprisonment for debt, despite its drab and dismal history, has been described as a triumph for the common law.[23] It has also been deplored, and some seventeenth-century men viewed it as being part of the tyranny of the Norman yoke.[24] An inadequate solution for all concerned, the exclusive nature of imprisonment virtually forced the creditor to relinquish other means of obtaining his money.[25] If the plight of debtors was a favorite theme with writers, equal attention was given to the frustrations of creditors who could not lay their hands on money and assets which were being spent to make prison bearable, even enjoyable, and to line the pockets of warders. Alternatively some prisoners had no money, and a man who might have been able to earn some cash to pay his debts was thus incapacitated.[26] The wretched state of prisoners was emphasized by Henry Brinkelow in a blast partly against "that abominable whore of Babylon (Rome I mean)," [27] and partly against many of the ills in English society. This tract, written in or around 1543, was almost contemporary with the first bankruptcy statute and may have been a reaction against it and other social legislation. Brinkelow, once a Grey Friar and now a mercer, inveighed against the practice of shutting up men without trial. He argued that to imprison a man until he died of starvation or disease was murder, and he asserted that prisoners were lodged like hogs and fed like dogs. Tudor prisons could indeed be so appalling as to make Dickensian circumstances appear a rest home. Yet if a prisoner had money—perhaps that ostensibly given him by friends and relatives—he might live in comparative luxury and freedom, provided that he was willing to pay through the nose. If a prisoner desired "to be in commons and to have a bed, he shall pay iiij times more for it than in the dearest inn in England." [28] A rich man could often pay for permission to leave the prison accompanied by a keeper and, although it is not known how far this was allowed in Henry VIII's time, it later became a crying, though doubtless exaggerated, scandal. William Leach, an agitator for law reform during the Interregnum, said that some debtors had traveled all over the country and had even, or so he claimed, gone to the East and West Indies. Some of these supposedly imprisoned debtors had met their creditors "and looked them in the face, and laughed at, and jeered them. . . ." [29]

The prison situation was appreciated by social thinkers who were already discerning a new morality with respect to the poor law, and who perhaps were well in advance of some lawyers with little understanding of Brinkelow's maxim that if a man "offend the law, let him have the law." Yet persistent criticism had only sporadic impact, and in general the unsavory situation continued unabated. Early in the seventeenth century, Dekker penned a description of London, almost a nightmare, conceived as a magic circle drawn by the cries of men, "all penniless, all prisoners."

> Let your eyes walk but over this paper and here survey is drawn. Upon one side of the Thames stand the White Lion, the King's Bench, the Marshalsea, the Clink, the Counter in Southwark; on the other side the Gatehouse, Ludgate, Newgate, Wood St[reet] Counter, Poultry Counter, Finsbury, New Prison, Lob's Pound and the Hole at St. Katherine's. Fourteen Golgothas environing one city! Fourteen charnel houses where men are buried alive! Either this must proceed from much cruelty in the creditor or much deceit in the debtor.

Nothing was done, and the bankruptcy statutes were in fact irrelevant to prison conditions and misuse. The machinery of constraint, as with law reform in general, would have to wait until the nineteenth century, and even then change was slow and miserly.[30]

It is probable that imprisonment for debt and other factors may have made flight appear more attractive in the early Tudor period than it had been previously. This does not mean that it was novel—some English merchants apparently fled abroad in 1414 and doubtless did so at other times—but there had been better ways of evading creditors.[31] Prior to the Henrician statute, flight did not carry that kind of construction which it did at some places on the continent, but it did invite outlawry. This implied forfeiture to the crown, and it was therefore of little benefit to creditors. Certainly, the assumption in 1543 was that too many had found resort in flight. One instance, possibly well known at the time, was the flight in 1535 of Antonio Guidotti. This man, son-in-law of Thomas Cromwell's client, Henry Huttoft, claimed that he was unable to meet bonds entered into on Huttoft's behalf. Guidotti returned, and in 1540 Huttoft begged Cromwell, who had been trying to arrange a settlement, to prevent his

---

22 *Ibid.*, pp. 42, 45, 108, 117.

23 Costigan, p. 106, n. 14.

24 Margaret James, *Social Problems and Policy During the Puritan Revolution* (London, 1966), p. 327.

25 Costigan, p. 90.

26 Prisoners often claimed that they could have paid their debts if allowed another six months. James, p. 329.

27 Later generations would not need the explanation.

28 H. Brinkelow, *The Complaynt of Roderyk Mors*, Early English Text Soc. (1874), pp. 27–30. Francis Alford's complaint of 1585 about the imperfections of the legal system noted the plight of prisoners. Lansdowne 44, ff. 2–13. Others commented on the "joyous" life of imprisoned "bankrupts." Lansdowne 99: ff. 185–186.

29 W. Leach, *Proposals for an Act for the More Speedy Satisfaction of Creditors* (London, 1649), pp. 3–4.

30 Brinkelow, p. 27. Dekker, *Lanthorne and Candle-light*, pp. 273–274.

31 Treiman, p. 232.

son-in-law from leaving again until some money and a release on a house in Southampton had been obtained. Guidotti spent some time in the Fleet prison and was temporarily deprived of his rights as a burgess. John Huttoft, Guidotti's brother-in-law, would sit as a member of Parliament for Southampton in the Parliament of 1541–1544 which passed the first bankruptcy statute.[32]

The other assumption in 1543 was that there had been an increasing tendency for debtors to keep to their houses. The pert belief that an Englishman's home is his castle is little more than a popular reference to a legal doctrine of commanding importance. The practical situation was that a debtor—together with such money, property, and valuables that he could gather around him—was virtually inviolate inside his own house. It was almost impossible to break in for the purpose of executing civil process, let alone for seizing assets, although these might not have been paid for. It was noted at the end of Elizabeth's reign that a sheriff, charged with executing a *fieri facias,* could not break through an outside door in order to secure entry, whereas if that door was already open he could force doors within the house and investigate chests in order to seize goods. Indeed if he failed to do this, an action would lie against him.[33] Not many lurking debtors can have left their outer doors unbolted. At times the courts were able to circumvent the situation. Due service of Chancery process in the late years of the sixteenth century could be achieved if the writ was hung on the door. This in itself was an acknowledgment that the server lacked authority to force the door, and that the person sought might be living in a place other than his normal residence. Failure to appear would be contempt of court and the offender might eventually be apprehended. This sort of thing was of little value to creditors, anxious for reimbursement and apprehensive as to what might be going on between the debtor and other creditors.

The 1543 statute, concerned as it was with aspects of insolvency and sequestration, had some antecedents. An early statute of Henry VII against fraudulent alienation tried to limit the availability of sanctuary and other privileged places.[34] A bankruptcy bill reached second reading in the House of Commons during the Reformation Parliament.[35] Perhaps most important was that statute of 1532 which regulated the taking of statutes staple. Staple jurisdiction and independence, already eroded, was now largely taken away, and where it survived remained merely as a forum for recovering small debts. The mercantile community was now almost fully exposed to the normal operations of the common law. Hence, it may be speculated, the traditional evasions of that law had to be adopted, and this may explain the contemporary supposition that flight and keeping to one's house had increased.[36]

The eventual legislation of 1543 grew out of a bill which was carried over from the session which ended in April of the previous year. This "Act Against Such Persons As Do Make Bankrupt" [37] began with a preamble which, in the words of a later authority, might serve a bankruptcy act today: [38]

> Where divers and sundry persons craftily obtaining into their hands great substance of other men's goods do suddenly flee to parts unknown or keep their houses, not minding to pay or restore to any their creditors their debts and duties, but at their own wills and pleasures consume the substance obtained by credit of other men, for their own pleasure and delicate living, against all reason equity and good conscience. . . .[39]

The lord chancellor, the lord treasurer, the lord president,[40] and the lord privy seal, together with other members of the Privy Council and the two chief justices, might order the imprisonment of debtors behaving in the indicated fashion. A distribution was to be arranged, the creditors being reimbursed proportionately according to the amounts owed. Action could only be taken after a written complaint had been made to three of the specified officials, provided that one was the lord chancellor, the lord president, or the lord privy seal. The nature of the estate, property, and effects liable to such action was outlined. Apart from chattels, debts, goods, wares, and other merchandises, the statute applied to annuities, fees, lands, offices, and tenements. The designated authorities—the work would devolve upon commissioners, but this was not stated—were empowered to search, view, rent, appraise, or sell any of these items to the benefit of the creditors.[41] Basil Montagu, writing in the early nine-

[32] G. R. Elton, *Reform and Renewal* (Cambridge, 1973), pp. 116–117. *L. and P. Henry VIII,* viii, no. 878; xii (1), no. 513; xv, no. 385. I am grateful, for these references and other information, to Dr. Mary Robertson of the Huntington Library. C. Platt, *Medieval Southampton: The Port and Trading Community, A. D. 1000–1600* (London, 1973), pp. 242–245. A. A. Ruddock, *Italian Merchants and Shipping in Southampton, 1270–1600* (Southampton, 1951), p. 249.

[33] 1 Brownl. & Golds. **50** (1602).

[34] 3 Henry VII c. 4. *Reeves' History of the English Law,* ed. W. F. Finlason (London, 1869) **3**: p. 290, n. (a).

[35] *L. and P. Henry VIII,* vi, no. 120. Elton, p. 149.

[36] 23 Henry VIII c. 6. Elton, pp. 148–149. Rich, p. 141. London and its merchant community had, and continued to have, a local system for payment of debts, proceedings for debt, seizure of assets—including those locked in warehouses—and compositions. A. Pulling, *A Practical Treatise on the Laws, Customs and Regulations of the City and Port of London* (London, 1842), p. 167 *et seq.*

[37] 34 and 35 Henry VIII c. 4. S. E. Lehmberg, *The Later Parliaments of Henry VIII, 1536–1547* (Cambridge, 1977), pp. 171, 181.

[38] Remington **1**: p. 6.

[39] 1543, *1.

[40] For this position, see G. R. Elton, *The Tudor Constitution* (Cambridge, 1960), pp. 92–93.

[41] 1543, *1.

teenth century, thought that this was contrary to law and justice because it introduced "the forcible and then unknown power of seizing a debtor's property and person by a summary process for the security of his creditors." [42]

A bankrupt could be summoned by proclamation and outlawed if he did not appear within three months "or as soon after as he conveniently may." [43] This allowed for the difficulties of distant traders and presumably gave the absentee, assuming that he heard about the proclamation, time to explain himself in writing and arrange a date for his return. Otherwise, there were few concessions. Bankrupts could be imprisoned. Yet new powers were not provided to deal with traditional defenses of persons who kept to their houses. This may be reflected in an Elizabethan complaint made by some French merchants.

> The English merchant . . . has this privilege, that when he has bought goods and intends to become a bankrupt, he can retire into his house, or even into his shop, provided that the door is closed with a lock or some barrier; and the bailiff cannot touch his goods, nor can anyone disturb him nor demand any account from him, nor arrest him or even talk to him, even though the poor ruined creditors may see the bankrupt in his house, with his wife, his factors and servants, publicly selling their goods in front of their eyes, without being able to attach these goods or any of the debtor's real or personal property.[44]

The 1543 statute tried to prevent creditors from cutting each other's throats. A temporary apportionment by rate was to be enforced and the ability of creditors to take advantage of every available remedy, including private negotiation with the bankrupt, was suspended, not extinguished, for an unspecified time. The bankrupt's liability was not reduced. He was treated as an offender, and hence the statute has been described as "quasi-criminal." His body, lands, and goods were liable to any valid recovery once creditors had received their ratable share of available assets. Creditors, who were not "fully satisfied and paid or otherwise contended," might subsequently seek satisfaction through all the remedies available at law.[45] The situation would revert to that described by Brinkelow as "first come, first served." [46] A bankrupt would then be at the mercy of his creditors despite the apparently bare cupboard of resources available for restitution. The only restriction was that which barred creditors from recovery against assets distributed by virtue of actions taken under authority of the statute.[47]

Some stipulations of the statute dealt with third persons. Anyone suspected of possessing a bankrupt's effects could be summoned and required to make disclosure. The penalty for concealment was a fine, amounting to double the value of the effects concerned, which was to be applied to the benefit of the creditors. A similar penalty was to be levied on creditors who attempted to obtain undue preference from the debtor after the action constituting bankruptcy, or who made approaches outside the procedures allowed by the statute. Collusive recoveries against bankrupts in fraud of creditors were roundly condemned and forbidden.[48]

Insofar as this statute departed, however weakly, from some traditional limitations which had raised a protective fence around debtors and even creditors, there was a need to cover those authorized by it. This was especially so with respect to men who acquired, by purchase or assignment, the goods and lands of the debtor.

> And that every direction order bargain sale and other things done by the said lords authorized as is aforesaid, in writing signed with their hands by authority of this act shall be good and effectual in the law to all intents constructions and purposes against the said offenders their heirs and executors for ever, as though the same order direction bargain and sale had been made by the said offender or offenders at his or their own free will and liberty, by writing indented enrolled in any of the King's courts of record.[49]

Otherwise, apart from general statements, adequate coverage was not really given to those who would execute the provisions of the act. This reflects the failure of the statute to establish much of a procedure beyond the stated requirement of petitioning the lord chancellor and others. Commissioners were not mentioned, and in consequence their position was weaker than it need have been.

The 1543 statute poses a problem for the historian in that the word *bankrupt* was only used in the title.[50] Thereafter mention was made of "divers and sundry persons." In distinct contrast to later statutes, reference was not made to those who lived through buying and selling by way of merchandise. The preamble mentioned "goods" and "houses," but in specifying acts of bankruptcy the statute did not refer to their sale, and it did not mention shops. Assets available to seizure included not only those associated with trade but also landed estates, rights over land, and offices. There is an ambiguity here which is reflected by later commentators.

Cowell indicated that the Henrician statute covered the taking of other men's goods, but he did not, in this context, bring up the subject of merchants and

[42] Montagu, p. 7.
[43] 1543, *5.
[44] Cited Treiman, p. 234.
[45] 1543, *4, 6.
[46] Brinkelow, p. 41.
[47] 1543, *6.
[48] 1543, *2, 3, 4.
[49] 1543, *1.
[50] I am grateful to Mr. H. C. Cobb and Mr. D. Johnson of the House of Lords Record Office for their assistance. In looking at the original statute, I have concluded that both the title and its endorsed form on the reverse side are probably contemporary with the text.

traders.[51] Spence, writing in the nineteenth century, assumed that the Elizabethan statute (1571) "confined" bankruptcy to those who used the trade of merchandise in gross or by retail, language which may indicate that he believed the earlier statute to have been broader in its coverage.[52] Some authorities have accepted that the 1543 act applied only to commercial men,[53] but as Jenks pointed out it "was not, in terms, confined to merchants." [54] Certainly, if read literally, we would have to presume that men other than merchants and traders were included. If so, this legislation reflected a principle which was not to be incorporated into the system of bankruptcy proceedings stemming from 1571 until three tortuous centuries had passed. The Elizabethan statute applied only to those who were merchants or exercised the trade of merchandise, or sought their living through buying and selling. Hence Blackstone's description of a bankrupt as "a trader, who secretes himself, or does certain other acts, tending to defraud his creditors." [55]

The 1543 statute poses some problems. The evidence of subsequent commissions is scattered and nebulous. One possibility is that the word *bankrupt*, although only mentioned in the statute's title, was already understood to have a particular meaning. Prior to 1543, bankruptcy may have acquired a specific association with trade. However, the term would continue to be used in a pejorative sense as in Edward Hall's mid-Tudor description of Warbeck's forces: "some bankrupts, some false English sanctuary men, some thieves, robbers and vagabonds. . . ." [56] Other legislative proposals of the Henrician period may indicate a differentiation according to occupation and status.[57] It was suggested in 1535 that "merchants shall employ their goods continually in traffic and not in purchasing lands." Four years later, there was a notion that merchants might be prevented from buying lands above a certain value. This kind of thinking was also current in 1559, when Elizabeth's first Parliament met. One idea was that merchants should not be allowed to purchase more than £50 *per annum* of inheritance, whereas aldermen and sheriffs of London might buy up to the value of £200 *per annum* because they approached the degree of knighthood.[58]

[51] T. Cowell, *The Interpreter* (1637), *sub tit.* "Bankrupts."

[52] G. Spence, *The Equitable Jurisdiction of the Court of Chancery* (Philadelphia, 1846, 1850) 1: p. 198. However his use of the word *confined* seems to represent a confusion in the relationship between the two statutes.

[53] Teevan and Smith, p. 253.

[54] E. Jenks, *A Short History of English Law* (London, 1949), p. 383.

[55] Blackstone 2: p. 284.

[56] *Hall's Chronicle*, ed. of 1548 (London, 1809), p. 472.

[57] See also W. S. Holdsworth, "The Development of the Law Merchant and its Courts," *Select Essays in Anglo-American Legal History* (Boston, 1907) 1: p. 327, n.1.

[58] *L. and P. Henry VIII*, ix, no. 725; xiv (1), no. 655. *H.M.C. Hatfield* 1: p. 163. Acknowledgment is due to L. Stone, "The Political Programme of Thomas Cromwell," *BIHR* **24** (1951): pp. 1–18. Stone's general argument was countered by G. R. Elton, "Parliamentary Drafts, 1529–40," *BIHR* **25** (1952): pp. 117–132. More recently, see Elton's *Reform and Renewal.*

The Henrician statute is also noteworthy in that it did not make an overt distinction between aliens and nationals. Presumably aliens could be both bankrupts and creditors, but this was not stated. Foreign merchants claimed exemption and they were not directly embraced by the 1571 statute. This was resented by English merchants who were themselves subject to bankruptcy laws in the Low Countries and elsewhere.[59]

The 1543 statute was riddled with inadequacies and uncertainties. The Privy Council, whose members had been mentioned, helped at times and occasionally intervened on behalf of creditors.[60] A more cogent possibility was that the lord chancellor might develop a jurisdiction in Chancery similar to that which in Elizabethan times he seemed to be assuming over marine insurance. It was natural to utilize Chancery powers since the lord chancellor was a leading official named in the statute, and since commissions were appointed under the Great Seal. It may be that through such assistance the 1543 statute, despite its weaknesses, did provide some sort of basis for operations against bankrupts.[61]

The Henrician statute was not abrogated by that of 1571. Cowell was quite right to begin his summary of bankruptcy law with a comment on the act of 1543.[62] The point is often confused. Holdsworth, for example, remarked that the first statute had been "replaced" by the Elizabethan one.[63] Coke's employment of loose language—he remarked that the 1543 statute was "altered" by later legislation—may have helped in the creation of a false impression.[64] Miscon-

[59] P.R.O., S.P.12/146, no. 125 (? *circa* 1580), "Touching the Right that Strangers have to Partake of Bankrupt Goods with English Creditors." The text of this document, which centers upon the Low Countries, may explain some of the difficulties which faced those who framed the 1571 act: "At the making of the said law by common report the strangers then resident in London being dealt with in that behalf utterly refused to be subject to any such law. . . ."

[60] *APC* 1552–1554, pp. 116, 250; 1554–1556, p. 344.

[61] W. J. Jones, "Elizabethan Marine Insurance: The Judicial Undergrowth," *Business History* **2** (1960): pp. 53 *et seq.* See below, p. 41. An example of Lord Chancellor Heath trying to help out in difficult circumstances is in P.R.O., S.P.11/11, no. 11 (1557).

[62] Cowell, *sub tit.* "Bankrupts."

[63] Holdsworth **8**: p. 237.

[64] Coke, *Fourth Institute*, p. 277. One editorial comment on Coke's *Reports* inaccurately asserts that the 1571 statute "wholly superseded" that of 1543. 2 Co.Rep., 25a, n. (B), **76** *English Reports*. The notion that the first statute was "altered," itself misleading, survived to be repeated in later works. See M. Bacon, *A New Abridgement of the Law*, rev. B. Wilson and J. Bouvier (Philadelphia, 1852) 1: p. 628. Spence's use of the word "confined" (see above, n. 52) suggests that he too misinterpreted the force of the 1571 statute. Scott rightly observed that an act was passed to "amend" the ex-

ception was probably aided by the fact that after 1571 little use seems to have been made of the earlier statute. Since the 1624 act applied the Elizabethan system equally to both aliens and nationals, it could be imagined that Henrician legislation had expired. It was not mentioned. Yet a later seventeenth-century commentator, Billinghurst, reported that though in his time the Henrician statute was "out of use" he did not "find it actually repealed," and he thought it not "altogether superfluous to take note of it." [65]

Theory apart, there is practical evidence that the Henrician statute was occasionally used after 1571. In February, 1595, a commission was granted by Lord Keeper Puckering and Chief Justice Popham with respect to the bankruptcy of two partners—Thomas Crumpe, a vintner, and William Worsoppe, a mercer, both of London—who were said to owe at least £1,300. Their creditors were seven English merchants and six merchant strangers. The 1543 statute, it was noted, "provided as well for strangers as for Englishmen to recover their just debts and duties to them due and owing in such cases as are therein expressed." [66] Later, cheek by jowl with an example of a petition and commission under the statutes of 1571 and 1604, the clerk of the crown in Chancery copied into his precedent book for the years 1603–1608 an example of a commission granted according to the Henrician statute. The petition from two merchant strangers had been made to Lord Chancellor Ellesmere, the chancellor of the Duchy of Lancaster, and the chief justice of the Common Pleas with respect to the bankruptcy of Zacharie le Pie of Chichester.[67] Likewise, in the early years of James I, there was the complicated affair of Matthew de Renzi, merchant stranger of Bishopgate, who was made a bankrupt despite his claim to have a prior protection. Large sums and rival groups of creditors, national and international, were involved. He fled to Ireland, claiming to be honest and ascribing his difficulties to others who had gone broke.[68]

There is reason to doubt if the Henrician statute was very effective, and commissions must have been infrequent after 1571. It was poorly worded and few could hope for a successful conclusion. Nonetheless, it had provided a novel means of proceeding, and some of its provisions were suggestive of later practice. It embraced the principle that absconding or defecting debtors should be punished, and it initiated a range of procedures which included the power to summon and examine third parties suspected of concealing property. Above all, it established the notion that creditors shared a community of interests. Since it was axiomatic that all should be reimbursed on an equal basis, the bankrupt's property was to be seized by a common agent and thereafter there was to be a distribution *pro rata* of the proceeds. Holdsworth's conclusion that it was essentially an attempt to prevent frauds on creditors is still valid.[69] This theme was fundamental to future legislation. "These statutes of bankruptcy are favorably to be construed for the creditors, being made for the suppression of fraud." [70]

III. ELIZABETHAN AND EARLY STUART STATUTES AND COMMISSIONS

Some assumptions of the Henrician statute were included in the 1571 act. Coupled with new ideas and Jacobean amendment, the principles and procedures for bankruptcy then established satisfied few. Garret de Malynes, commenting on the provisions of 1571 and 1604, thought that there were grounds for praise but that really dishonest men could "prevent the means of suing for the same." The intention of the statutes could be broken "as easily as a spider's web." [1] This was also the opinion of Dekker. The problem was in part one of detail, and some improvement was made in 1624. Even so, hindsight tells us that most leading principles of later bankruptcy law, with the exception of the discharge and voluntary bankruptcy, had already been introduced.

There were economic and financial worries in 1571, but legislation probably stemmed primarily from disquiet about existing procedures. Other factors merely worked to give this disquiet a hearing. Bankruptcy bills had been introduced and made some progress in 1563, the year of the great apprenticeship statute, and in 1566, when Elizabeth had made a hasty termination of the session.[2] Nonetheless, a re-examination of the bankruptcy laws was always most likely in periods of commercial anxiety. In 1571, as Parliament met, some prophesied that all trades connected with buying and selling were in danger of rapid decay. A list of bankrupts—nineteen of the forty mentioned concerned London—emphasized the number of industrialists, merchants, and tradesmen who had lost

---

isting law relating to bankrupts, but he was silent on both the nature of the law and the nature of the amendment. W. R. Scott, *The Constitution and Finance of English, Scottish, and Irish Joint-Stock Companies to 1720* (Cambridge, 1912) **1**: p. 53. Even the P.R.O. *Guide* perpetuates error by stating that the statute of 1543 was "repealed" by that of 1571. *Guide to the Contents of the Public Record Office* (London, 1963) **1**: p. 166. However, not all recent descriptions are inaccurate. Halsbury (**2**: p. 251) merely notes that the 1543 statute was "followed" by subsequent legislation.

[65] G. Billinghurst, *All the Statutes now in Force and Use Concerning Bankrupts* (London, 1695), p. 105.

[66] El. 5525.

[67] P.R.O., C.193/5, no. 80. Professor M. Pulman kindly checked this reference for me.

[68] *H.M.C. Hatfield,* **17**: pp. 593–594; **18**: pp. 10, 24, 239, 323; **19**: pp. 69, 76; **24**: pp. 53, 55.

[69] Holdsworth **1**: p. 470.

[70] Goodinge, p. 34.

[1] G. de Malynes, *Lex Mercatoria* (London, 1686), p. 157.

[2] *CJ* **1**: pp. 68–69, 70, 72, 74–75, 79–80.

their credit. The abuses and deceits of "bankrupts" were described as intolerable. The existing machinery of law was seen as weak, and there was a demand that Parliament must act.[3]

This sense of urgency cannot be separated from other concerns. Legislation against fraudulent conveyances, certainly a related matter, was approved.[4] The bill against defaulting tellers was passed.[5] During a famous debate about usury and in other discussions, members of Parliament talked about the evils of bankruptcy, debt, luxurious living, overspending, and usury. There was little satisfaction with a 1563 statute which had attempted to limit the availability of credit for the purchase of imported apparel and goods.[6] The new usury statute may have been crucial. Except for the period, 1545–1552, the taking of interest had been forbidden, and it has been suggested that this may have restricted the use of borrowed capital in the wool trade. If a more permissive approach was now to be allowed, it may well have been supposed that this would encourage borrowing and therefore necessitate a more stringent control of mercantile and trading debts.[7] Indeed many of these bills can be regarded as constituting a packet of proposed legislation.

In 1571 the bankruptcy bill, along with that against fraudulent collectors and receivers, was among the first to be considered by the upper house. It was sent down, engrossed on parchment, with a message recommending expedition. This was on May 16. The House of Commons concluded that in view of the consideration given to the matter by the Lords, there was no need on their part for either engrossment or the striking of a committee. The first reading was received on 17 May, the second on the twenty first, and the third three days later.[8]

Intimations of prosperity, encouraged by the revival of Anglo-Flemish trade in April, 1573, marked the decade, but in 1581 there was an attempt to clarify some difficulties in the bankruptcy law which had come to light. A bill brought from the Lords survived its second reading in the Commons before being "dashed" upon the question.[9] The advantageous trend petered out in the 1580's, formal war with Spain broke out, and the mid-1590's were exceptionally bad: harvests failed, the real value of wages fell dramatically, and the textile industry all but foundered. In 1601, Parliament considered a bill against "cozening bankrupts and lewd apprentices and factors." This was notable because of its harsh tone and because it associated together three different categories of malefactors. It was proposed that bankrupts should be treated as embezzlers unless there was positive evidence that financial difficulty resulted from bad debts or losses at sea. A first reading was obtained on 14 December, but the bill did not proceed. Dissolution was imminent, as the House of Commons had been warned on 10 December by the queen. Urged by Elizabeth to speed up business, the members of Parliament were more concerned with other matters, in particular a bill against the transportation of ordnance which government spokesmen seemed determined to obstruct.[10]

When the first Parliament of James I met in 1604, it was possible to be optimistic. The worst moments of the 1590's had passed, and the war was over. On the other hand plague had made its mark, and there was the usual worry about that perennially ailing mainstay of the economy, the cloth trade. An act intended to eradicate some imperfections in the bankruptcy system was passed, but this legislation was not as harsh as that proposed in 1601.[11] In 1610 the subject came up again. Some members of Parliament accused Salisbury, the lord treasurer, of having damaged trade through his extension of impositions and suggested that he was therefore responsible for a number of bankruptcies. Salisbury was probably justified in dismissing this as speculation. In any case, this argument was only incidental to the great debates then under way.[12] A bankruptcy bill was introduced in 1614, but there could be no progress in this brief "Addled Parliament." [13] Subsequently, problems which had not been perceived when the 1604 act was passed attracted attention as the general trade prosperity of James's first decade, itself unspectacular,

---

[3] Lansdowne 13, ff. 54–55. The largest claim, against a bankrupt of unspecified occupation from Buckinghamshire, was for £6,000. Scott 1: p. 53. Neale, *Parliaments, 1559–1581*, p. 219. For failures in London during the 1560's, particularly that of Sir Thomas Lodge, see G. D. Ramsey, *The City of London in International Politics at the Accession of Elizabeth Tudor* (Manchester, 1975), pp. 57–59, 239.

[4] 13 Elizabeth I c. 5.

[5] See above, p. 7.

[6] Traders were supposed to insist upon payment in cash unless the customer had £3,000 *per annum*. 5 Elizabeth I c. 6. In 1559, it had been proposed that bankruptcy be made a felony. *H.M.C. Hatfield* 1: p. 164.

[7] 13 Elizabeth I c. 8. P. J. Bowden, *The Wool Trade in Tudor and Stuart England* (London, 1962), p. 100. A bill for usury was proposed in 1604 and one against pawnbrokers passed (1 James I c. 21); bills for both bankruptcy and usury were considered in 1621. The act for usury, passed in 1624 (21 James I c. 17), also tightened up controls on the activities of brokers and scriveners. In this respect, note the title of the 1624 bankruptcy statute. *CJ* 1: p. 204. *Commons Debates 1621* 7: pp. 209–210.

[8] *LJ* 1: pp. 670, 672, 685, 687. *CJ* 1: pp. 90–91, 92. S. D'Ewes, *A Compleat Journal of the Votes, Speeches and Debates . . . Throughout the Whole Reign of Queen Elizabeth* (1693), pp. 184, 186.

[9] *CJ* 1: pp. 133–134. If the document noted above (Chap. II n. 59) can indeed be assigned to 1580, then it is possible that there had been some intention of meeting complaints about foreigners.

[10] P.R.O., S.P.12/283, nos 22, 23. J. E. Neale, *Elizabeth I and her Parliaments, 1584–1601* (London, 1957), pp. 421, 423.

[11] *CJ* 1: p. 236.

[12] *Proceedings in Parliament 1610*, ed. Elizabeth Read Foster (New Haven, 1966) 1: p. 131; 2: pp. 334, 403.

[13] *CJ* 1: p. 481.

expired with the Cockayne fiasco and the disintegration of peace in Europe. The whole period from the accession of James I to the Restoration "was not marked by conspicuous growth: on the contrary, it was a time of painful economic readjustment in a darkening European context." [14]

"I had rather be a plowman than a merchant," said a member of Parliament in 1621. All sorts of explanations were offered, but while many discussed the relationship between crumbling English cloth exports and the economic and monetary consequences of wars in Europe, few could agree on the exact causal connection.[15] Many remedies were suggested, and one of these—not unrelated to the attack upon Bacon's performance as lord chancellor—was a reshaping of the 1571 and 1604 bankruptcy statutes. Commercial crises intensified what many had said for years: the existing bankruptcy law was ineffective because the statutes were full of gaping loopholes. In other ways a lead had already been given in Scotland, where an act of the lords of Council and Session against unlawful dispositions and alienations of bankrupts, made in July, 1620, was ratified in 1621.[16] In England a bankruptcy bill, which provided for corporal punishment under certain circumstances, was introduced by Sir Francis Crane, a member of Parliament for Penryn. An extreme suggestion was that some bankrupts should be whipped to death. Sir Edward Coke felt that bankrupts might deserve this fate, but he did not like "laws written in blood." Wentworth and others expressed the real nature of current anger: many clothiers had failed and it was supposed that this was often due to the deceitful bankruptcy of their financial associates. It was said that clothiers were demanding a new act. Considerable progress was made, but nothing was achieved since this Parliament collapsed amid disagreement with the king on other matters.[17]

The depression continued. In 1622 it was reported from Suffolk that manufacturers had suffered great losses, in part because of bankruptcies.[18] By 1624, however, the political climate had altered. Prince Charles and Buckingham were in pursuit of diplomatic revenge and native popularity; as Cranfield fell a new bankruptcy statute was born. It was modeled upon the design of 1621, but excluded bloodthirsty suggestions. Even the proposal, put forward again, that bankruptcy should be made a felony was left out. It was, nonetheless, the most stringent bankruptcy statute, which had yet been produced. In other respects this Parliament, hostile to monopolies, sought a greater freedom—in terms of economic activity—for the landowner, the farmer, and even those who wished to participate in the cloth trade. This had little to do with the circumstances of tradesmen and most merchants. They might in some respects be allowed a greater freedom of enterprise and maneuver—the 1604 session of Parliament had also been marked by a campaign against certain company regulations—but this could entail a stricter set of regulations to satisfy a society of landed producers and investors.[19] Furthermore, there was still a backlash against the memory of Bacon's innovations and past interventions by the Privy Council.[20] An attempt to tighten the bankruptcy laws was not out of touch with the economic ethos of 1624.

Henceforth, and for a few decades, the initiative in providing refinement passed from Parliament to the judiciary. The latter could do no more than interpret complex problems as they arose. Political circumstances precluded legislation. This applies to all aspects of debt. In August, 1641, the House of Commons rejected a bill intended to aid creditors and relieve debtors unable to meet their obligations. The proposal concerned a field of contention much broader than bankruptcy, and there was little time in which to consider such matters.[21]

It would be several decades before the existing bankruptcy statutes were revised. In the meantime, there were a multitude of judicial and occasionally executive explanations, interpretations, and modifications. Sometimes this was because of specific and immediate doubts brought to the notice of the courts by litigants. At other times general and social circumstances called for an evaluation, as when, in the early years of the Interregnum, commissioners of bankruptcy found that a debtor's estate had been sequestered because he had borne arms against Parliament. If the cause of sequestration had happened after the action of bankruptcy they might, with reasonable hope of success, beg that the sequestration be discharged. Alternatively, and this was most likely if the order of events was reversed, the commissioners might request a composition for the sequestered estate, perhaps paying the composi-

[14] C. Wilson, *England's Apprenticeship, 1603–1763* (London, 1965), p. xi.

[15] Supple, pp. 54, 58. It has been argued that contemporaries who hesitated to put the war high on their list of causes for the depression may not have been far wrong. J. G. Gould, "The Trade Depression of the Early 1620's," *Ec.HR*, 2nd ser. 7 (1954): pp. 81–90.

[16] *The Acts of Parliaments of Scotland* 4: pp. 615–616. G. Mackenzie, *Observations on the 18 Act 23 Parliament, King James VI* (Edinburgh, 1675).

[17] *CJ* 1: pp. 532, 537, 551, 575, 626, 632. *Commons Debates 1621* 2: pp. 162, 211, 267; 5: pp. 176, 266, n. 1, 457, 505; 6: p. 182. M. Prestwich, *Cranfield: Politics and Profits under the Early Stuarts* (Oxford, 1966), pp. 304–305.

[18] Supple, pp. 52 *et seq.* E. M. Leonard, *The Early History of English Poor Relief* (Cambridge, 1900), p. 148.

[19] *CJ* 1: pp. 684, 694, 751, 779, 782. *Commons Debates 1621* 3: p. 296. Wilson, p. 54. In any case, although one clause referred to "bodies politic or corporate," the monopolies statute excluded London, corporate towns, corporations, and fellowships. Carr, p. lxxii.

[20] See below, pp. 40, 45–48.

[21] *CJ* 2: p. 277.

tion fine. The property could then be disposed of to the benefit of the creditors.[22] These were exceptional times, but the value of composition had been stressed and this might be of service in the future.

BANKRUPTS

Under the statutes of 1571 and 1604 English subjects, born or denizen, could commit an act of bankruptcy.[23] Aliens, a significant minority in the business community, were ignored but not directly excluded. Hence Englishmen feared, as a member of Parliament put it in 1621, "that strangers may transport themselves and [their] estates beyond [the] seas."[24] Aliens were specifically brought into the system both as bankrupts and creditors in 1624.[25] This statute also included scriveners, as had been propsed in 1621.[26] These men were important because like brokers—familiar in the world of finance but not mentioned in the statute—they engaged in incipient forms of banking. They traded in money, and their failure or dishonesty could have widespread repercussions. Here again bankruptcy legislation must be related to that concerning usury: the 1624 usury act noted scriveners and prescribed imprisonment for those who took more than the proper rate of interest.[27] There is evidence that scriveners had previously been declared bankrupt, but this had clearly been open to question.[28] Similar exigencies doubtless explain an order of 1645 that those responsible for rendering accounts were to be treated as bankrupts if they were in prison or absent for one month.[29]

The statutes were progressively explanatory. Initially it was stated that persons using the trade of merchandise—by bargaining, exchange and selling—were covered, as were those who sought their trade or living by buying and selling.[30] However, the introductory statements of 1604 and 1624, unlike that of 1571, did not specify merchants as such. This raised a question of law upon the construction of the statutes themselves, and this is one area in which it is more than ordinarily impossible to draw a general rule from particular cases. The point, for example, has been made that using an act of merchandise is common to every man. Every person buys and very often he sells as well, though this is less frequent. The implication of the statutes was that those covered must sell as well as buy as a means of living. Distinctions were difficult to determine, and we should not expect consistency. By and large, however, there were two developments. Over several decades, the application of these statutes was slowly limited to men and women who can be described as merchants and traders, and it was gradually assumed that they did not apply to landed persons. Second, by close interpretation of the words, specific means of living were indicated as being covered by the statutes. Even so, it was possible for one baker to be within the statutes whereas another was outside.[31]

One of the fascinations of bankruptcy is the way in which it compelled judges and lawyers to grope towards their own definitions of some social distinctions. In particular, there was the problem of determining what a gentleman was, the more so as it tended to be assumed that such a being could not really live by buying and selling. The statutes had said nothing about gentlemen. Certainly there was plenty of contemporary advice. A gentleman, it was said, should be taken for a gentleman or spend his money like a gentleman. He was "one who can live idly and without manual labor, and will bear the port, charge and countenance of a gentleman."[32] At times the debate, or rather the series of debates, could seem remote from reality. Was it possible to be a gentleman in one sense and yet to live by buying and selling? At first sight it would seem that in many cases the answer could only be positive. Furthermore, successful men who had risen in trade, or their sons, bought their way into land and later into landed society. Nor was it uncommon for younger sons to seek careers in trade, although subsequently they might revert to the habits and manner of country gentlemen.[33] The perennial problem of younger sons was related to primogeniture, a practice which was not legally required with respect to the devise of lands. John Earle wrote about the misfortune of younger sons of gentlemen denied the means to maintain that status but expected to live up to their birth. Withdrawal to the Low Countries or marriage to a rich widow often represented the last

[22] *Cal. Committee for Compounding Cases: Domestic, 1643–1660* pt 2: pp. 1019, 1099; pt 3: pp. 2351-2352; pt 4: p. 2501.

[23] 1571, *1; 1604, *1.

[24] *Commons Debates 1621* 5: p. 176; 7: pp. 104–108. By 1611, it had been decided that aliens could be made bankrupt, although they could not be petitioners. Hence an action of words lay. In any case, the allegation was damaging and there was, of course, the Henrician statute. Bulstrode, 134–135, Tirlot v. Morris; Yelverton, 198.

[25] 1624, *2.

[26] 1624, *2. *Commons Debates 1621* 7: p. 105.

[27] 21 James I c. 17, *2.

[28] In 1596 a commission issued with respect to John Deane, scrivener of Holborn, who had gone broke for over £4,000. El. 5370. Scriveners were unique in that they were specifically mentioned in the 1624 statute. Hence, Nottingham would insist that a bankrupt scrivener should be named as such and not simply be described as a tradesman who lived by buying and selling. *Nottingham's Cases* 1: p. 314.

[29] *Acts and Ordinances of the Interregnum, 1642–60* 1: p. 720.

[30] 1571, *1; 1604, *1; 1624, *1, 2.

[31] See the analysis in *Petersdorff's Abridgement* (New York, 1829) 3: pp. 315–320. There is a separate and very different story concerning interpretation of "exercising a trade" with respect to the Elizabethan statute of artificers (1563). However, in some cases this statute was used to determine whether a man was a trader and thus within the bankruptcy laws.

[32] Cited Wilson, p. 112.

[33] *Ibid.*, p. 10.

refuge. Some drifted into trade. This, as Edward Chamberlayne noted, could be managed without apprenticeship, but it seems that a number were in fact apprenticed to merchants.[34]

The difficulties implicit in the situation began to trouble the courts in the latter part of James I's reign. In 1620, the Chancery was confronted by a man who had been born a gentleman but made his living through buying and selling iron and similar transactions. A Chancery master, advising that the bankruptcy statutes seemed to apply, admitted that he had doubts "because it is a new case, and wanteth precedents, and concerneth a gentleman of good family, bred in another course." [35] There were many who occupied a gray area, such as the Cheshire person who described himself in 1640 as "a gentleman by birth and a linen draper by trade." [36] However, the judges were not directly concerned with social assumption and they were not asked to define the nature of a gentleman. Their task was to determine if a person gained his living by buying and selling and whether his transactions were comprehended within the meaning of the bankruptcy statutes. Thus a farmer, gentleman or otherwise, bought and sold, but he sold more than he bought in the way of business, and he was, anyhow, working his own estate. It followed that he was not embraced by the statutes. A number of distinctly commercial means of livelihood were likewise held to be excluded.[37]

Early adventurers into Virginia or Greenland, in contrast to Muscovy merchants, were not within the statutes. It was held that although they exchanged "trifles" with "the savages" their main concern was with plantation and discovery.[38] An important distinction was that eventually made between investment and active participation in commerce. Guidelines in this respect were not easily established and they did not exist before 1640. The critical case was that of Sir John Wolstenholme, a stockholder in the East India Company and formerly a prominent figure in the city of London, who was alleged to have gone bankrupt in or around June, 1646, to the tune of over £2,000. A bankruptcy commission was issued in July, 1650, and its membership was reconstituted in May, 1652. This was maintained in 1653 even though Wolstenholme had lands worth £3,000 *per annum* and it could not be established that he obtained "the greatest part of his living by buying and selling." All this was considered as being overshadowed by his work as an active member of the East India Company and its managing committee. After years of hesitation, the impact of this decision could have been cataclysmic: not least because some law reformers had castigated the inefficiency of laws which did not apply to debtors of all classes. Instead, the Restoration confirmed trends which are perhaps discernible during the Protectorate. The "Act Declaratory Concerning Bankrupts" of 1662 confronted the fact that persons "not bred up to trade" became members of public companies. In respect of their stock, members of the East India Company, the Guinea Company, and the "Royal Fishing Trade" were specifically excluded from liability under the bankruptcy statutes. The Wolstenholme decision was declared contrary to law and voided.[39] The supposition that members of a chartered company might not be declared bankrupt in respect of their stock was from the beginning extended by statute to shareholders of the Bank of England.[40]

In 1661, the reissued charter of the Levant Company had accorded a distinct position to contributors of capital and directors who might have little other connection with practical trading activities. It was stated that members of the company must be freemen of the city unless they lived within twenty miles of London and were "noblemen and gentlemen of quality who never were apprentices to, nor bred in, nor have applied themselves to any course of trade as their calling." [41] Such a stipulation, so important to the history of company development, reflects upon the financial involvement of aristocrats, gentlemen, lawyers, and other classes or professions in England's commercial expansion. It also reflects the long-existing gulf between great merchants and craftsmen or retailers. On the other side of the coin, it was decided by the second half of the seventeenth century that a chartered company could not be held liable in respect of the bankruptcy of one of its members. This was often stated as an important justification when a charter was being solicited; otherwise "the stock will be liable to the particular and private debts of the sev-

[34] J. Earle, *Microcosmography* (London, ed. of 1897), pp. 22–24. E. Chamberlayne, *Angliæ Notitia or the Present State of England* (2nd ed., London, 1669), pp. 444–445. Joan Thirsk, "Younger Sons in the Seventeenth Century," *History* **54** (Oct., 1969): pp. 358–377.

[35] Monro, p. 286.

[36] Wilson, p. 14. Of course, many general matters concerning status and honor were determined in the court of chivalry.

[37] Hutton, pp. 46, 49–50; 3 Mod., 328–331, Newton v. Trigg (1685).

[38] J. Stone, *The Reading upon the Statute of the Thirteenth of Elizabeth, Chapter 7, Touching Bankrupts* (London, 1656), p. 42.

[39] P.R.O., C.67/81, no. 11; C.67/83, no. 70. 14 Charles II c. 24. For some details on the Wolstenholme family, see T. K. Rabb, *Enterprise and Empire: Merchant and Gentry Investment in the Expansion of England, 1575–1630* (Cambridge, Mass., 1967), pp. 173–174. At this time, the Guinea and East India Companies were unique in their fiscal structure. Elsewhere each individual traded on his own account and thus, it was pointed out, could go bankrupt even if a gentleman. 2 Keble, 487, Cotton v. Daintry (1669). The Royal Fishing Company was incorporated in 1664.

[40] 8 and 9 William III c. 20, *47.

[41] Carr, p. xli, n. 9. The immediate purpose of this provision was to protect London by forcing merchants to take up freedom of the city. A. C. Wood, *A History of the Levant Company* (Oxford, 1935), p. 95.

eral partners and subject to be torn to pieces upon the bankruptcy of any of them." [42] In all this the judges played a part; across the seventeenth century their rulings assume considerable significance. However, cases that have been reported often center as much upon usage of the word *bankrupt* as upon the statutes.

Holdsworth warned that one of the most inadequate types of case law is to be found in that growing around the interpretation of words,[43] but judges over a long period do appear to have done their best by adhering to a narrow kind of logic. Many cases required them to decide whether a person could become a bankrupt. Most of these, although contrivance may be suspected, were not ostensible challenges to bankruptcy commissions which had been sued out. The question was whether use of the word *bankrupt* and other language constituted scandalous words. The phrase "knavish bankrupt" was often cited, and in the reign of James I it was ruled that "bankrupt knave" could be construed as two substantives and therefore might be scandalous and actionable. In most cases, it was necessary to decide if the person claiming to have been slandered was capable of becoming a bankrupt under the statutes. If he was, the words were heinous, damaging and scandalous. Malynes summed up the position: "so that to call a decayed gentleman a bankrupt (although he have had dealing in the world) beareth no action at the common law, unless he were a merchant or shopkeeper, etc." [44]

Before the end of the sixteenth century, it had been decided that it was actionable to call a shoemaker a bankrupt because he obtained his living through buying and selling.[45] This was clarified in the reign of Charles I when it was argued that a shoemaker lived by his credit as much as by his labor. As a corollary, it was stressed that those who lived only by manual labor—for instance, husbandmen and laborers—could not be brought within the statutes.[46] Similar reasoning was applied to other men and their crafts. In the reign of James I, for example, it was decided that a dyer was a trader within the meaning of the statutes.[47] The plaintiff in one action for words argued that he bargained and sold lead, but the defendant said there was no proof that this was the plaintiff's trade or that it constituted his means of living. In any case, he was styled as a gentleman. Nonetheless, it was decided that an action lay, and an Elizabethan decision was cited to the effect that a tanner could have such an action.[48] Soon after it was made clear that all points had to be established. Buying and selling were not enough. It had also to be shown that this activity constituted both the trade and the livelihood of the complaining party.[49] Inevitably this approach allowed of many variations. In the middle of the seventeenth century, it was understood that the statutes applied to innkeepers,[50] but it was later decided that these should be excluded. An innkeeper who put an unreasonable price on the goods which he sold to travelers would be committing an offense which came within the jurisdiction of the justices of the peace. Although he bought things, he did not sell them in such a fashion as to become a trader. Furthermore, unlike a dyer or a shoemaker, he did not work with other men's goods in the normal sense. He did not buy and sell by way of contract, but for a price made his lodging, comfort, and provisions available to travelers.[51] In 1697 these principles were again confirmed, and it was repeated that farmers were not traders within the meaning of the acts. Soon after an old principle was underlined when it was predictably ruled that an infant could not be made a bankrupt because his debts were voidable: "no man can be a bankrupt for debts which he is not obliged to pay." [52] In this case the judges had taken a direct look at a bankruptcy problem, but in most situations their intervention, as it affected interpretation of the bankruptcy statutes, was subsidiary to the principal issue in dispute.[53]

[42] Carr, pp. xvii–xviii, ci–cii. In the nineteenth century, members were still liable for the debts of their company, but a careful distinction was made between the individual and the company. Bankruptcy of the company was not to be construed as the bankruptcy of any member. For this and later developments of the nineteenth century, including the position of shareholders and the role of Chancery, see C. A. Cooke, *Corporation, Trust and Company* (Manchester, 1951), pp. 139–140, 146–151, 161–163, 172.

[43] Holdsworth **5**: pp. 206–207.

[44] Cro. Jac., 345, Selby v. Carrier (*ca.* 1614). D. Mellinkoff, *The Language of the Law* (Boston, 1963), p. 175. Malynes, *Lex Mercatoria,* p. 157.

[45] Cro. Eliz., 268, Stanley v. Osbaston (*ca.* 1592).

[46] Cro. Car., 31, Crumpe v. Barne (1626). Goodinge, p. 12.

[47] Cro. Jac., 585, Squire v. Johns (1620). A dyer had previously had a bankruptcy commission awarded against him. El. 3543.

[48] Hutton, 46, Allen v. Swift (1621). There was question in another case whether indeed a tanner could have an action for the words, "thou art a bankrupt knave." 1 Brownl. & Golds., 16, York v. Cecil (1616). In 1652, a bankruptcy commission was issued with respect to a tanner of Derby. P.R.O., C.67/83, no. 29.

[49] Hutton, 49–50, Hawkins v. Cutts (1622). Occupations cannot be put into neat categories. One favorite example of the times was provided by bakers. Generally these were within the statutes, but a person could be known as a baker and largely work as a baker and yet be excluded because the trading element was not strong enough or because the work was actually subsidiary to the means of livelihood, as in the case of a servant in a large establishment.

[50] Stone, *Reading,* p. 43. P.R.O., C.67/81, no. 31 is a commission with respect to the bankruptcy of an "innholder" of Essex.

[51] 3 Mod., 328–331, Newton v. Trigg (1685). See Cro. Car., 549–551, Crisp v. Pratt (1635).

[52] 1 Ld Ray., 286–287, Meggot v. Mills (1697); 443, Rex v. Cole (1699–1700).

[53] There were a host of these decisions which grew in number from the Restoration. A summary is to be found in 2 Co. Rep., 25a, n. (B), 76 *English Reports.* A survey was provided by Goodinge, pp. 166–175.

Women appear as bankrupts, occasionally as partners but more commonly as widows who had assumed a shop or trade. Furthermore, a commercially active wife might have a distinct position under the custom of London: a majority of Common Pleas judges did not accept the proposition that she was construed by law to be the servant of her husband. For by the custom it was possible for her to be a *feme sole merchant*: "the *feme* trades by herself in one trade, with which her husband doth not meddle, and buys and sells in that trade." [54]

ACTS OF BANKRUPTCY

A person could only become a bankrupt if he behaved in a fashion specified by the statutes, and if his creditors opted to follow a procedure allowed by this legislation. It was always, if reluctantly, recognized that men might be unfortunate—bad debts and losses at sea were favorite examples—but this had nothing to do with it. The nature and size of the debt, unless it was small, was irrelevant. Bankruptcy followed from a particular kind of action committed by a definable man in a stipulated situation. The occupation of the debtor and the act of bankruptcy were equally important. Thus in the middle of the seventeenth century, bankruptcy commissions usually specified that the debtor employed himself in merchandise by way of bargaining and exchanging, and that he had gone bankrupt with the intent of defrauding and hindering the petitioning creditors.[55] Intent was always important. The debtor might commit one of the stipulated actions and yet claim that it was fortuitous.

According to the 1571 statute, a person could be declared bankrupt if he left the country, otherwise absented himself, kept to his house, sought sanctuary, was arrested for debt "or other thing not grown or due for money delivered wares sold or any other just or lawful cause or good consideration or purposes," was outlawed, or departed from his house with the intention of defrauding creditors. Clearly these conditions were often in need of interpretation, and they probably provided the principal basis for early disputes at law. The charge that a debtor kept to his house, for example, had to be proved by consistent behavior. Unless the intent was to commit bankruptcy or to defraud creditors, one who retreated behind his doors to evade certain types of process but subsequently went out was not a bankrupt. Likewise, a number of cases determined that a trader might be consistently unavailable at his house, but he had not committed an act of bankruptcy if he continued to appear and be seen in such central trading places as the Exchange.[56]

That the descriptions given in 1571 were insufficient to embrace the variety of situations which might arise was tacitly acknowledged by the 1604 statute. The list of circumstances then given, together with verbal modifications, may provide a clue as to some of the difficulties which had occurred.[57]

In 1604, there was a greater concentration upon fraudulent behavior. The phrase "yield him or herself to prison" was employed in both statutes, but it was now clear that conniving at one's own arrest or procuring the attachment and sequestration of one's goods were actions constituting bankruptcy. Imprisonment for six months on account of debt was to be construed as revealing that kind of dishonesty which justified bankruptcy proceedings. Equally important was the simple statement that a fraudulent grant or conveyance of lands, tenements, goods, and chattels constituted an act of bankruptcy. The 1571 statute had only specified punishment for those who fraudulently acquired the debtor's assets before or after the act of bankruptcy.[58]

If we are to believe Dekker and Malynes, granted that the former talked about bankrupts in a loose fashion, the statutes so far had failed abysmally. Dekker made strident comments on the futility of legislation passed in 1543, 1571, and 1604. He was incensed at the way in which the broad and high-sounding preamble to the Henrician act, which in its wording should have eliminated the scope for scoundrels, seemed to count for nothing. This time considering the wiles of the crafty rather than the calamity of the unfortunate, he described how "politic bankrupts" manipulated both the bankruptcy laws and imprisonment for debt itself. A "man-eater" could defeat descriptions of an act of bankruptcy by locking himself in his house and yet making judicious appearances. He would barricade his lair with double locks, triple doors, invincible bolts, and pieces of timber, yet emerge to sell "the goods of his neighbor before his face without blushes." As for imprisonment, that had become a form of refuge.

> Strong and cunning nets were spread by those Parliaments to catch these foxes. Yet how many of them have been since, and at this hour are, earthed in the King's Bench, the Fleet and that abused sanctuary of Ludgate! Here they play at bowls, lie in fair chambers within the Rule, fare like Dives, laugh at Lazarus, can walk up and down many times by *habeas corpus* and jeer their creditors. There they lie barricadoed within King Lud's bulwark against gun-shot; there they strut up and down the prison like magnificos in Venice on the Rialto, brave in their clothes, spruce in ruffs, with gold-wrought night-caps on their heads. They feed deliciously, plenteously, voluptuously,

[54] Cro. Car., 68–69, Langham v. Bewett (1627).

[55] For example, P.R.O., C.67/77, no. 2. The bankrupt was a fishmonger of London.

[56] 1571, *1. Cro. Eliz., 13 (1582). In 1613, a newly chosen chamberlain of Bristol was dismissed. This man, "being indebted and behind hand by losses at sea, was fain to keep house at St. James's Fair following for debt." *Merchants and Merchandise in Seventeenth-Century Bristol*, ed. P. McGrath, Bristol Rec. Soc. (1955), p. 173.

[57] 1571, *1; 1604, *1.

[58] 1571, *1, 6; 1604, *1.

have excellent wines to drink, handsome wives to lie with when they please, who come in not like the wives of prisoners but of the best and wealthiest citizens. These men command the stone walls, not the walls them.

Dekker was colorful, but unlike some other critics of prison life he commented directly on the bankruptcy statutes. His tirade illustrates the swell of public anger and the feeling that hitherto statutory description of acts of bankruptcy was so inept that proceedings could not even be begun in many cases. This was the lengthy background to the second Jacobean statute, that of the king's last Parliament. Something would be done along the desired lines, and this would be the basis for bankruptcy proceedings until the end of the century. The revisions as first sight seem tepid and unsatisfactory, as doubtless they were, but the presumed increase in the number of bankruptcy commissions sued out by and after the Restoration may indicate that some sinew had been added to the rules.[59]

In 1624, previous descriptions of acts of bankruptcy were repeated and extended. In particular, the statute mentioned procurement of protections and attempts to get creditors to accept compositions whereby they either took less than was due or conceded further time for payment. These provisions were blows against the Privy Council and some courts, especially Chancery, but it was still quite proper for debtors to arrange meetings with creditors prior to debts becoming due in order to solicit licenses for further time or other arrangements. This would not be an act of bankruptcy since neither fraud nor the intent to defraud was present.[60] Other circumstances included failure to pay, or an attempt to compound for, a debt of £100 or more six months after it was due, or arrest for such a debt. An act of bankruptcy had also occurred if nothing was received within six months of a writ to recover debt being sued out with proper notice, or if the debtor stayed in prison for two months on this or any other action for debt. A person arrested for debt—again this was to be £100 or more—who escaped or obtained some sort of bail was to be adjudged a bankrupt, the state of bankruptcy beginning from the time of the original arrest. Thus was it hoped to bar much of the in-and-out usage of prison as a sanctuary to evade bankruptcy which Dekker had deplored.[61]

INITIAL PROCEDURE

The lord chancellor alone was authorized to issue commissions of bankruptcy under the Great Seal and to appoint "such wise and honest discreet persons as to him shall seem good." He would do this on receiving a complaint or petition in writing.[62] The practice developed, certainly during the Stuart period, that this must be accompanied by an affidavit that debts were owed—from 1624 the specific sum of £100 or more had to be mentioned—and that an act of bankruptcy had been committed.[63] The petitioning creditors would suggest the names of possible commissioners in a separate document, and these would be listed by the clerk of the commissions for the benefit of the lord chancellor. After names had been deleted or added, the petition and docket were returned to the clerk who then engrossed a commission on parchment for the seal. In the seventeenth century, petitioning creditors were required to enter bonds as to the veracity of their claim that the debtor was a bankrupt. This, although not automatic, was probably also done in the Elizabethan period.[64]

In selecting and adding names, lord chancellors prior to the 1630's probably tried to avoid using the same people on too many occasions. There was also the danger, as Nottingham later pointed out, of "worthy" men being named, perhaps to give credit to the commission, and yet not attending the proceedings.[65] During Puckering's lord keepership in the 1590's, most commissions seem to have numbered seven persons with a quorum of four, but some numbered nine with a quorum of five. Some smaller commissions were appointed but this was unusual, and indeed Puckering seems to have increased the membership of many suggested commissions from five to seven. The commission, as it finally appeared, often contained a number of people, for instance members of the debtor's own company, who might be expected to deal fairly with him.[66] However, the prime purpose was to employ men who were familiar with the debtor, his holdings, worth and trade. One commission was altered because the men appointed lived rather far away from the bankrupt.[67] All the creditors of Christopher Gaunt, a chapman of King's Lynn, were members of London companies, but the commission was made up of five men from King's Lynn, including the recorder, together with Nicholas Hare

[59] Dekker, *Sinnes of London*, pp. 23–24; *Lanthorne and Candle-light*, pp. 275–276. Other writers were equally critical. In 1618, Geoffrey Mynshul described prisons as "your bankrupt's banqueting house" where debtors made themselves "galley-slaves only to wear golden fetters." D. Veall, *The Popular Movement for Law Reform, 1640–1660* (Oxford, 1970), p. 14.

[60] 1624, *2. Goodinge, p. 28. This was an affirmation of common business practice, if properly conducted.

[61] 1624, *2.

[62] 1571, *2. The occasional complaint was made to the queen and forwarded to the lord chancellor. *CSP Dom.* 1581–1590, p. 271.

[63] Goodinge, p. 2.

[64] P.R.O., E.333/17. When demanded, the minimum sum was usually £200, and this became standard from 1619. Sanders 1, i: p. 122. Nottingham once demanded £500. *Nottingham's 'Manual'*, p. 163.

[65] Sanders 1, i: p. 122. *Nottingham's 'Manual'*, pp. 163–164.

[66] El. 4092, 4093, 4271, 4279, 4395.

[67] El. 5392.

of Stoebarden, Norfolk, and a solitary London merchant.[68] In another case, three merchant tailors were included in the commission although all the creditors followed that trade.[69] Aldermen, businessmen, and gentlemen made up the bulk of commissioners appointed in the 1590's. On occasion, a scrivener was appointed.[70] Legal talent included local recorders, serjeants-at-law, and persons such as William Aubrey, Julius Caesar, and Henry Hobart.[71] William Mill, clerk of the Star Chamber, was appointed to one commission, and Mr. Justic Clench was selected when Thomas Dedham of Ipswich went broke.[72] Francis Bacon, as lord chancellor in 1619, directed that someone learned in the law must always be included, and there is evidence to suggest that this became more or less the rule.[73]

At least up to the 1630's, there does not seem to have been much departure from late Elizabethan practice. A typical commission might include three barristers and four "attorneys" (the use of this word did not carry the usual connotation, and the men so described were gentlemen or merchants).[74] However, by the outbreak of the civil war, and probably before, commissions tended to be smaller, numbering five or even three, and lawyers were less noticeable. This was apparently because a slate of regular or professional commissioners had emerged, those who would be condemned by Leach as "monopolizing commissioners and officers, or so pretended. . . ."[75] Between 1642 and 1654, the events of war and Interregnum making little difference to the pattern, some names come up repeatedly: John, George, and William Norbury, members of a Chancery clerical family; Anthony Boys, George Cotton, and John Penrice. In other words, the situation was that which a few decades earlier may have been deemed undesirable.[76] It was usual to specify one of these men as a member of the quorum although others might also be named to the commission. This is most apparent with respect to bankruptcies in London and its environs. On occasion, the commission included one of the regulars but indicated that he was to be a sleeping partner. John Penrice mostly appeared on London commissions, but in the case of a Bristol mercer he was placed second on the commission to John Wentworth, Esq., who was to do the actual work. The implication is that the regular panel had a financial interest in the work of bankruptcy commissions. It must be supposed that the emergence of these men is closely related to the growth of an administrative organization surrounding the issue and documentation of commissions.[77]

Once the commissioners had been appointed, the next task was to find the bankrupt. Since his nonavailability—usually he was described as being "late" of London or some other place—was often the occasion for proceedings, this might be no more than a formality. In these circumstances, the 1571 statute required the commissioners to ensure that a proclamation was made in the appropriate market place on five market days. Nonappearance placed the bankrupt outside royal protection, and his helpers and concealers were to be fined and imprisoned.[78] Under the 1604 statute lawful warning was to be left in writing on three occasions at the place where the bankrupt, his wife and family had normally lived or lodged during the previous year. After failure to appear, the commissioners were to send a precept to the relevant local officials—for instance, the bailiffs of Southwark—requiring them to make proclamation on five market days. If the bankrupt still did not come in, he could be arrested by warrant of the commissioners wherever he was found, "in place privileged or not."[79] This phrase was ambiguous. Election to the House of Commons as a device to frustrate creditors was not unknown. Bacon, replying to the speaker's request for privileges in 1621, said that freedom from arrest was granted but the king trusted that the House would be "moderate in granting their protections." It was "a great abuse to justice, a distaste to his Majesty, a scandal to themselves, and a wrong to their creditors, for them to countenance bankrupts, and by that means to free dishonest men from the arrest of such as were truly damnified by their bad dealing."[80] Whatever members of Parliament may have thought about the lord chancellor's own leniency towards some debtors, they were still worried about evasions of the bankruptcy statutes. It was proposed that those who failed to appear—a neglect described as worse than burglary or highway robbery—should be treated as felons and face a possible death penalty. A

[68] El. 3558.

[69] El. 3998.

[70] El. 3429.

[71] El. 4072, 4395, 4871, 5370.

[72] El. 3991, 4279.

[73] Sanders 1, i: p. 122. Malynes confirms the extensive use of lawyers. *Lex Mercatoria*, p. 158. However, Bacon's order may indicate that the legal element had been declining or questioned. See also *Nottingham's 'Manual'*, p. 163.

[74] P.R.O., E.333/17.

[75] Leach, *Proposals for an Act*, p. 17.

[76] P.R.O., C.67/76a-85.

[77] P.R.O., C.67/83, no. 25 (1652).

[78] 1571, *8.

[79] 1604, *4. W. West, *The Second Part of Symboleography* (London, 1618), sect., 154–159.

[80] Bacon was probably using the word *bankrupt* in its popular sense. The problem posed by debtor members of Parliament, who were for a time able to evade their creditors, was an old one. Little had been done to improve the situation by the eighteenth century. L. B. Namier, *The Structure of Politics at the Accession of George III* (London, 1957), pp. 55, n. 1, 59–61. Namier may have used the word *bankrupt* where *debtor* would be more appropriate. For the position of peers, as later explained, see 1 Atk., 201, *ex parte* Meymot (1747); 4 George III c. 33.

variety of such proposals, made in both 1621 and 1624, found no place in the legislation of the latter year.[81]

It is probable that nearly all bankrupts, appearing of their own volition or apprehended, were imprisoned. If, however, a bankrupt's behavior was reasonable, he could subsequently be licensed to move about freely in order to assist in the settlement of his affairs and debts. Before this freedom could normally be granted, the first task of the commissioners was to examine creditors and other witnesses in order to establish the facts: whether the debtor's living and trade brought him within the statutes, the nature of the alleged act of bankruptcy, and the structure of his debts and obligations. If sufficient facts were proven, the commissioners would declare the debtor to be a bankrupt. The debtor, however, might deny that he had committed any such act, challenge the petitioners' version of his debts, or argue that he was not a trader within the meaning of the bankruptcy legislation. At least with respect to the latter point, it seems that in the early Stuart period he might file a *caveat* against grant of the commission or petition the lord chancellor to suspend an awarded commission by *supersedeas* until the point was decided. Nottingham recalled having seen a note that a commission had once been granted solely to determine whether the debtor was a bankrupt, but he concluded that such limited commissions were improper. In the 1640's, it seems to have been decided that the commission ought to be granted and doubts or questions tried upon the commission. This was in accordance with the implications of some rather indirectly worded clauses of the 1604 and 1624 statutes. It clearly was intended that the commissioners were to prove the debtor's status and make a declaration of bankruptcy. On the other hand, it seems that by the end of the seventeenth century they tended in their wording and pronouncements to be increasingly cautious. Rather than risking actions against themselves, despite the ground rules for such established in 1604, it may even be that they welcomed initiative from interested parties which left the fact of bankruptcy to trial at law. This could be achieved in many ways, possibly after distribution had commenced. Thus Goodinge noted, for example, that any execution on a judgment that debt was due could be stopped by alleging that a commission of bankruptcy had been issued against the successful plaintiff. Having chosen this course, the assignee of the commission had to take out a special *scire facias* or bring an action of detinue on the judgment to try whether or not the man was a bankrupt.[82]

---

[81] P.R.O., S.P.14/160, no. 74.

[82] Goodinge, pp. 48, 62, 106. Noy, 140, Edward's Case (n.d.). Monro, p. 286. *Nottingham's 'Manual'*, pp. 161–164. 1604, *11; 1624, *13.

CLERKS AND OFFICIALS

The lord chancellor was authorized to issue bankruptcy commissions but none of the statutes indicated who was to do the clerical work. It was probably assumed that the task could be delegated. After 1571 the work was done by Jasper Fisher, one of the Chancery six clerks. Fisher died insolvent after building a house in London equipped with "gardens of pleasure, bowling-alleys and the like," which became known as "Fisher's Folly."[83] Later in Elizabeth's reign, responsibility was assumed by Thomas Powle. This decrepit but influential official held several positions in the court of Chancery including those of a six clerk and clerk of the crown. On his death, the job was granted by Lord Keeper Egerton to Bartrobe Lukin, but early in the reign of James I this was challenged by the new clerk of the crown, George Coppin.[84]

Coppin claimed that the clerk of the crown in Chancery, as a minister of the court of Parliament, was vested with the right to make all commissions created by statute. Lord Keeper Nicholas Bacon, said Coppin, would not have allowed Jasper Fisher to do this work if he had been aware of the rights and responsibilities of the clerk of the crown. He dismissed as a fabrication Lukin's argument that Lord Chancellor Hatton (1587–1591) had given this responsibility to one of his followers. In fact the real difficulty was posed by Powle's career. He had continued as nominal clerk of the crown although he had conveyed responsibility to a deputy, a surrender so complete that the *House of Commons Journal* sometimes refers to that deputy as "clerk of the crown." Bankruptcy commissions, however, had been engrossed in Powle's six clerk's office and this seemed to suggest that the work was considered to be distinct.[85] It is difficult not to feel some sympathy for the tenor of Coppin's arguments, but events since the 1571 statute were against him. Egerton's inquiry into Chancery fees, ordered in 1598, treated the clerk who made out bankruptcy commissions as a distinct official. This independence was to be maintained, although the position was again at times associated with the clerk of the crown.[86]

The dispute may help to explain the failure to enroll bankruptcy commissions noted by William Lambarde in 1596. Other commissions were also not being enrolled, but bankruptcy commissions were not included by name in the 1599 Chancery order listing commissions which should henceforth be enrolled.

---

[83] Monro, p. 343.

[84] El. 2955, 2956.

[85] El. 2954–2957, 2999. W. J. Jones, *The Elizabethan Court of Chancery* (Oxford, 1967), pp. 130–134.

[86] *Parliamentary Accounts and Papers*, 1830–1831, viii (1), p. 25. H. C. Maxwell-Lyte, *Historical Notes on the Use of the Great Seal of England* (London, 1926), pp. 272, 280–281.

Uncertainty over responsibility and fees may have been a factor.[87]

Administrators involved in the issue of bankruptcy commissions were subjected to close scrutiny by commissioners authorized to inquire into fees during the 1620's and the 1630's. According to the 1598 inquiry into Chancery fees, the cost of obtaining a bankruptcy commission was in part rated upon the valuation of those goods for which the debtor had gone broke. There was a minimum charge of two shillings, and additional fees included two shillings for the seal and two shillings and four pence for enrollment. These costs were justified by Lukin on the grounds that preparation of commissions involved labor out of all proportion to the paucity of their number.[88] Lukin was probably responsible for establishing a fee of £4 13s. 4d. for making the bill, preparing the docket of the commission for engrossment, and securing the seal. However, James I granted an office to John Latch and Humphrey Bradbourne. The work was done by their deputy, Matthew Colborne, who had a position in a six clerk's office and was also deputy for the office of writing patents of denization. He probably took over the clerical work involved in the issue of bankruptcy commissions, and he was accused in the early 1630's of allowing the basic fee to rise to £5 10s. 0d.[89]

Another position, that of examiner and register of commissions of bankruptcy, created in 1618, was granted to Edward Hawkins with reversion to Christopher Colby and further reversion to the son of Hawkins. The senior Hawkins worked through a deputy, and the office was established in Ivy Lane, St. Paul's. This creation by letters patent was criticized, not least because of the uncertainty surrounding fees and gratuities. Yet the office can probably be regarded as more helpful than malign. King James said that he was advised by Bacon and other experts, and it was said that there had been confusion in the keeping of bankruptcy documents and proceedings, with resulting difficulties for persons who were "aggrieved." [90] This was a typical apologia for the creation of a new office, and the list of advisers mentioned calls to mind the referees attacked in the 1621 Parliament. In this instance, however, there seems to have been some justification. It is doubtful if the clerk who issued bankruptcy commissions had been able to handle subsequent challenges or the need of persons to whom goods had been assigned to establish their titles.

The new office was responsible for most of the necessary paper and procedural work for commissions executed within the city of London and its suburbs. This included proclamations and warrants of appearance, apprehension, and summons; the drawing and writing of interrogatories and the taking of depositions; the drawing and engrossing of indentures of assignment and schedules, provision of copies, and much other work. This list of responsibilities gives some indication of practical matters outside the scope of statute. Clerks were appointed, and by 1638 the office had passed to John Booker, who, like his predecessors, worked through a deputy, John Bolles. The need for commissions to be made public as soon as possible, so that creditors would receive notice, had been put forward as an argument for the creation of this register. In practice the effective deputy was expected to attend meetings of commissioners, and he became an expert and adviser on procedures.[91] Despite objections, this office was described as very "commodious" to the public by one who wanted similar arrangements to be made for the rest of England. Charles I granted a patent in March, 1639, for the creation of an office to deal with bankruptcy commissions executed outside the metropolitan area, but this was revoked in the following month.[92] Despite contortions of policy, a beginning had nonetheless been made toward a division between the London area and the rest of the country which was to be a feature of bankruptcy proceedings in the eighteenth century. Perhaps this distinction received an impetus during the Republic, when commissioners for imprisoned debtors in the metropolitan area were required to act as though they were commissioners of bankruptcy. If so, it also means that an attempt was being made to breach the wall between bankrupts and other debtors. It was stated that those imprisoned for debt

[87] P. L. Ward, "William Lambarde's Collections on Chancery," *Harvard Library Bulletin* (1953) **7**: p. 281 and n. 40. Sanders **1**, i: pp. 80–82.

[88] *Parliamentary Papers*, p. 25. Sanders **1**, i: p. 141. El. 2957.

[89] *CSP Dom.* 1619–1623, p. 12. P.R.O., E.215/1/2/23; E.215/2/224, 225, 226. In August, 1632, the office for executing the laws and statutes against bankrupts was renewed to John Latch and Thomas Jennys. *D.K.Rep.* **48**, App.: p. 462.

[90] P.R.O., E.215/3/235. During James I's reign, various proposals dealing with bankruptcy matters were put forward by projectors. *Commons Debates 1621* **7**: 469 n.1.

[91] *CSP Dom.* 1611–1618, pp. 539, 567. P.R.O., E.215/1/2/22; E.215/2/227; E.215/2/229, nos. 1, 2; E.215/3/232–235. It was established that this official was a sworn officer of Chancery, constantly attendant on the court, and thus possessing all the privileges due to that position. This meant, among other things, that he was privileged to sue and be sued in Chancery insofar as the court had jurisdiction. Sanders **1**, i: p. 141. Publication of commissions was sometimes delayed, and so creditors did not receive immediate notice. *Nottingham's 'Manual'*, p. 164.

[92] *CSP Dom.* 1640–1641, p. 356. W. H. Price, *The English Patents of Monopoly* (Cambridge, Mass., 1913), pp. 171, 174. *Privy Council Registers* 1637–1645 (London, 1967–1968) **5**: p. 209; **10**: p. 438. Complaints in the reign of Charles II led to the appointment of an inspector who was also given responsibility for keeping commissions, depositions, and proceedings. The places "adjacent" to London and Westminster expanded to comprise Middlesex, Essex, Hertfordshire, Surrey, Sussex, Buckinghamshire, Berkshire, and Kent. Sanders **1**, i: pp. 354–355.

would become bankrupts unless they settled their accounts by 1 April, 1654.[93]

GENERAL POWERS OF THE COMMISSIONERS

Bankruptcy commissions were expected to obtain restitution for the creditors. The only concession made to the bankrupt was his right to receive an account, information about the disposal of his lands and goods, and delivery of anything which remained after the creditors had been satisfied.[94]

The 1571 statute empowered commissioners to apprehend the bankrupt's person and to dispose of his property to the benefit of the creditors.[95] This involved the seizure, valuation, and sale of chattels, effects, goods, lands, and movables, including cash and debts. Unless directly transferred to creditors, everything was to be sold for their benefit. One or two of the creditors would be appointed as overseers for this valuation, sale, and distribution.[96]

The most obvious difficulty was occasioned by one of the specified acts of bankruptcy: when a debtor locked himself in his house. The statutes of 1571 and 1604 gave inadequate guidance as to how the bankrupt and his property were to be seized. To open the door of a house implied the use of force, but this was not sanctioned. Hence the complaints of Dekker and that provision of the 1624 statute which empowered commissioners to break open the doors of houses and shops.[97]

The 1571 statute was weak in other ways. The commissioners were authorized to examine various persons,[98] but nothing was said as to the examination of the bankrupt himself. It seems that "secret" and "subtle" bankrupts refused to be examined. This anomaly was tackled in 1604. Bankrupts, refusing examination on interrogatories as to the whereabouts of their possessions, were henceforth to be imprisoned until they submitted. Perjury, to the value of £10 or more to the damage of the creditors, could bring the offender to the pillory. Here he was to stand for two hours with one ear nailed and then cut off.[99] This punishment was confirmed in 1624 and extended to bankrupts who were convicted of conveying or concealing property worth £20. Indictment was to be at the assizes or general sessions in the place where the debtor had become bankrupt.[100]

It took decades before commissions were given an effective authority for interrogation. The bankrupt himself might be acquiescent or apprehended, but under the rules of 1571 and 1604 little could be done about his wife, even though she might have concealed cash, jewelry, plate, and other property. It was ruled that examination of a bankrupt's wife to prove bankruptcy certainly was contrary to law. As a corollary it was noted that a wife, unlike a son, was not bound to "reveal" her husband's treason. However, the 1624 statute allowed her to be examined for discovery of assets.[101]

Other persons had always been liable to sworn examination about the bankrupt's effects, conducted in any style convenient to the commissioners. This implied that *viva voce* examination was acceptable, but written interrogatories and depositions were probably favored. Anyone who refused to be examined, who declined to disclose effects in his possession, or who fraudulently obtained effects, was liable to a penalty double the value of the goods. In 1571, however, guidelines were not given as to how examination might be compelled or a double penalty collected.[102]

Parliament in 1604 tried to remove difficulties which had restricted operation of the Elizabethan statute. Persons suspected of having a bankrupt's property were to be submitted to sworn examination on interrogatories. Recalcitrants could be arrested and imprisoned, without bail or mainprise, until they complied. Those suspected of perjury were to be prosecuted under the 1563 perjury statute. On the other hand, some consideration was shown: witnesses were to receive their costs and charges.[103] The ability of commissioners to examine was again strengthened in 1624.[104]

The powers of bankruptcy commissioners were terminated by the death of the sovereign, but late in the Restoration period it was decided that a new commission could work from the point where the previous one had expired.[105] This problem was not abnormal. Bankruptcy commissions were also faced by less regal forms of extinction. The 1604 statute permitted continuation of proceedings despite the death of the bankrupt.[106] It was later explained that the commission was nonetheless extinguished unless it had started work before the bankrupt died.[107]

There were other statutory weaknesses. Eliza-

[93] *Acts and Ordinances of the Interregnum* 2: pp. 753–754, 763.

[94] 1571, *4. 1604, *10.

[95] 1571, *2.

[96] West, sect., 154–159.

[97] 1624, *7. See above, pp. 24–25.

[98] 1571, *5, 6. See below.

[99] 1604, *4. Although not stated, conviction could possibly be under the perjury statute of 1563 which was mentioned in connection with the perjury of witnesses and others. 1604, *6.

[100] 1624, *6.

[101] 1624, *5. 1 Brownl. & Golds., 47 (1612). *Commons Debates 1621* 3: p. 296.

[102] 1571, *5. 1624, *8. Witnesses not involved as creditors could be examined. E.333/17.

[103] 1604, *5, 6.

[104] 1624, *8.

[105] 1 Eq. Ca. Abr., 52 (1687). Only altered by 5 George II c. 30, *45.

[106] 1604, *12. This presumably was from the date when the commission made a declaration of bankruptcy.

[107] *Nottingham's Cases* 1: p. 315. 1 Eq. Ca. Abr., 52 (1687).

bethan and early Stuart bankruptcy commissions, certainly before 1624, worked under some very severe handicaps.

CREDITORS

In most situations of debt there was bound to be suspicion among creditors, the fear being that some would come to terms with the debtor or with the administrators of an estate. One case, although not a matter of bankruptcy, illustrates the reality of this danger.

Magdalene Stoakes was the widow and executrix of a man who had left goods worth £5,000. This was supposedly sufficient to cover the testator's debts and legacies, but he had stood surety for several people. These combined with the widow to obtain judgments "by consent" at common law "of all the forfeiture[s] of the said bonds suffered (for the most part) by herself to incur, and for some others of which there was composition made in the life of the said testator, and for some after his death." In consequence "there were none of the creditors paid, but such only as the defendant, Stoakes, favored . . . whereas the complainant [in Chancery] with divers others were left unsatisfied of their due and lawful debts growing by like bonds and specialities." The executrix, indeed, had pleaded against an action of debt that she had insufficient assets to satisfy the debts claimed by those creditors who had not already made an agreement with her. Issue was reached, but before judgment a bill was exhibited in Chancery. The reason for this switch in tactics and courts was apparent. As William Lambarde put it, "the said recoveries will not be adjudged fraudulent at the common law, because the same were had upon just forfeitures in the eyes of that law" even though they had been "procured by combination and practice to the defeating of the testator's other due debts." The executrix had made "easy compositions with the creditors, that were parties to the fraud, which nevertheless will be taken for no fraud at the common law." Chancery, concluded Lambarde, could well be occupied "in examining these practices, the rather because many nowadays grow bold to commit the same, and such like, upon assurance that by the common law they are not to be touched therefore." [108]

Lambarde's report has been mentioned here because he clearly thought that a problem existed, and because in the search for solutions he was helping to inaugurate an approach which two decades later would have shattering consequences for Francis Bacon.[109] In the meantime, bankruptcy statutes were based upon the proposition that individual creditors should not benefit or receive back debts at the expense of other creditors. Coke, looking at the situation with a particular eye to the 1571 statute, pointed out that the intention was to

> relieve the creditors of the bankrupt equally, and that there should be an equal and ratable proportion observed in the distribution of the bankrupt's goods amongst the creditors, having regard to the quantity of their several debts; so that one should not prevent the other, but all should be in *æquali jure*.[110]

The commissioners were indeed authorized to make a proportionate division among the creditors.[111] However, they were plagued by creditors who, although they had joined in the commission, claimed priority on the ground of legal decisions and recorded bonds—valid forms of judgment—on which execution had not been sued out. Only in 1624, after the major crisis of 1616,[112] was statutory guidance provided. This took the form of a restatement that creditors joining in the commission must comply with the essential principle of equal division. This rule was to cover all judgments and bonds—including those of sureties—execution of which had not been sued out before the debtor committed his act of bankruptcy.[113]

A single creditor or group of creditors could petition for a commission. The first two statutes gave little guidance in these circumstances, but a convention de-

[108] P.R.O., C.39/24, Muschamp v. Stoakes (1598). The statutes against fraudulent conveyances might also help. Henry VII's statute (see above, p. 15) had voided fraudulent alienations by the debtor, but it needed subsequent legislation—notably the combined effort of the two 1571 statutes—to build some few fences against alienation for the benefit of others, notably favored creditors. Reeves 3: p. 291 n.(a). Hudson noted that "where a man being indebted to many will deliver his goods to the satisfying of one expecting relief from him, and so the rest are wholly unsatisfied, this delivery (although there were a just debt)" constituted a fraudulent deed within the meaning of 13 Elizabeth I c. 5. W. Hudson, "A Treatise on the Court of Star Chamber," *Collectanea Juridica*, ed. F. Hargrave 2 (London, 1792): p. 97. See below for problems of composition and conformity, pp. 45–48.

[109] See below, pp. 45–48.

[110] 2 Co. Rep., 25b.

[111] There was always concern that the bankrupt might get his friends to petition for a commission. These pseudo-creditors might, as Nottingham feared, "huddle up" the execution of a commission and so defeat the interests of other creditors. He proposed that petitioners should be required to provide an affidavit that they would prosecute the commission truly and *bonâ fide*, and affirm that they did not have any secret arrangements with the bankrupt. *Nottingham's 'Manual'*, p. 163.

[112] See below, p. 45.

[113] 1624, *8. Nottingham modified this position when he ruled that a plaintiff on a judgment could have an equity which outranked the equity of other creditors. This arose from a case in which a creditor had failed to join in a commission because he relied on a judgment and execution. The sum owed to him exceeded the total owing to other creditors, but the judgment was only acknowledged after the act of bankruptcy had been committed. Although the commission was closed, Nottingham secured an agreement whereby the single creditor could join in it, pay his share of the expenses, and yet keep what was already in his hands *pro ratâ* towards his own satisfaction. *Nottingham's Cases* 2: pp. 491–492.

veloped, confirmed in 1624, that those who exhibited a petition must be owed debts totaling at least £100.[114] In many cases, however, this sum was too trifling to have significance. At other times, the £100 claimed may either have been a fiction or may have included the total value of penalties as well as the actual capital debt. This was rather hard, as Nottingham took pains to stress, since a penalty was normally double the value of the debt.[115]

The 1571 statute did not deny the right of creditors to join in the commission after it had been sued out, but it failed to indicate how and when they could become associated. In 1604, however, it was enacted that creditors might join in the commission, thus sharing its costs and expenses, up to four months after it had been sued out. Thereafter the commissioners could start sharing out the proceeds.[116] In practice, it became understood that distribution might begin after four months. When this was not possible, commissioners would promise to give further time and provide notice.[117] At the very least, it had been ensured that commissioners devoted at least a third of a year to the consideration of their task, but much of this time must in any case have been spent in initial procedures and inquiries.[118] The statutes did not take direct notice of creditors who made no attempt to join in or who declined to do so. It is possible that those who remained outside cherished hopes of working through other means, perhaps the good offices provided by the Privy Council, and they may have tried to prevent a state of bankruptcy being declared. The 1624 statute, with the longest list yet of actions constituting bankruptcy, struck a blow at these creditors, and also at the crumbling authority of the Privy Council in matters of debt.[119]

Creditors regained their freedom of action when the commission was wound up. The bankrupt was not discharged from any remaining liability, and creditors could proceed individually against him at law and use any means of recovery available. This may have encouraged bankrupts to do their best to prolong the life of commissions. Some lasted for many years, and there were grounds for this in the 1571 reference to creditors who were not fully satified or "otherwise contended." [120] It is of course evident that some commissioners, possibly encouraged by higher authority, tried to get creditors to give further time for the remaining sums or even to express satisfaction, but such experimentation must in no way be confused with the notion of a discharge.[121]

PROBLEMS OF PROPERTY

The 1571 statute made the acts of commissioners valid against the bankrupt, his wife, heirs, assignees, and all persons who might claim by, from, or under him. It also covered lords of the manor from whom copyhold or customary lands were held. A protection was thus given to the disposal of property by the commissioners. This was clear enough. It was rather less easy to be certain as to the assets which could be disposed of, and this was especially so when these had been previously conveyed.[122]

It is possible that some inadequacies of the Elizabethan statute may have been due to hasty drafting and insufficient reflection by the House of Commons.[123] Apparently as an afterthought, an exception was annexed as a schedule to the original bill. This stated that a *bona fide* conveyance of lands or tenements made before the action of bankrupty was not to be questioned.[124] The 1604 statute tried to close loopholes.[125] All conveyances made before the action of bankruptcy were to be void, unless it could be shown that they had been made for good consideration and value, for example as part of a marriage contract. The onus of proof was in effect switched to the bankrupt and to those to whom he had conveyed.[126] A time limit was not provided, but the judges would warn creditors not to fasten upon deeds made long previous to an act of bankruptcy.[127] A period of five years may have become the yardstick.[128]

At this point, acts of bankruptcy and powers of recovery over property became fused. It was a chicken-

[114] 1624, *2. P.R.O., E.333/17.

[115] *Nottingham's Cases* 2: pp. 570–571.

[116] 1604, *2.

[117] Some commissions, after giving this promise, were accused of making a sudden distribution among a few creditors. Nottingham required commissioners to execute at a specified time and place, all of which was to be announced at least fourteen days before distribution. *Nottingham's 'Manual'*, p. 163.

[118] The four months could expire before some creditors were aware of what was going on (*ibid.*, p. 164), but it was supposedly adequate for sending notice even to those who lived in remote parts. Hutton, 37–38, Ruggles Case. There was nothing to prevent creditors from joining after the four months and initial distribution, but this was only with respect to any residue and cannot often have been advantageous. 2 Chan. Cases, 153–154, Harding v. Marsh (1683).

[119] See below, p. 40.

[120] 1571, *9.

[121] See below, p. 49.

[122] 1571, *2, 3. If the commissioners sold copyhold or customary lands, the purchasers had to satisfy the lord of his entry fine before admittance. Lands and chattels held by the bankrupt as feoffee to charitable uses were not his assets. For these and other problems, see G. Jones, *History of the Law of Charity, 1532–1827* (Cambridge, 1969), pp. 95–96. Money and goods, taken from a debtor on an extent a few days before issue of a bankruptcy commission, was not subject to distribution. Cro. Car., 149–150, Audley v. Halsey (1629).

[123] See above, p. 19.

[124] 1571, *11.

[125] This approach seems to have replaced the abortive attempt in 1601 to fashion a new and harsher approach towards bankrupts. See above, p. 19.

[126] 1604, *3.

[127] Hutton, 42–43, Cartwright v. Underhill (1617).

[128] See below, at n. 131.

and-egg situation insofar as the 1604 statute implied that an act of bankruptcy occurred if a grant or conveyance could be deemed as in fraud of creditors.[129] Basil Montagu argued that these words had a technical meaning in that they were confined to deeds, that is, instruments under hand and seal. Thus if a debtor executed a deed by which he conveyed one-twentieth of his property with the intention of favoring one of his creditors, he committed an act of bankruptcy, and this was what the statute intended. However, if he delivered all or part of his property by means other than deed, or executed a warrant of attorney by which the property might be taken, he did not commit an act of bankruptcy even if he was deliberately favoring one of the creditors. This, claimed Montagu, was "an apparent deviation from the original intention of the legislature." [130]

The 1624 statute was stringent, although from the viewpoint of commissioners and some creditors it may have been considered as faintly liberal. It established that purchases made for good and valuable consideration could not be impeached if five years passed between the act of bankruptcy and the petition to prove the man a bankrupt.[131] Was this an invitation? The statute also declared that goods in the actual possession of the bankrupt, by consent of the real proprietors, were liable to be distributed towards payment of the debts. It was argued, in explanation, that many persons, aware that they were going to become bankrupts, conveyed goods to other men on good consideration, although they kept them "and are reputed the owners thereof, and dispose the same as their own." [132] The commissioners were also empowered to sell lands, including those entailed, and action of this kind was to be valid against the heirs.[133] Commissioners might make a disposal of mortgaged estates which could be redeemed by the bankrupt.[134]

The situation with respect to assets acquired after the act of bankruptcy was clearer. Any lands or effects which came into the hands of the bankrupt, notably by reversion or inheritance, could be distributed by the commissioners during the life of the commission. The point should have been obvious, but even this item received a somewhat indirect wording in the 1571 statute, and it followed after that clause which allowed subsequent freedom of action to creditors.[135]

Bad debts were often the explanation for insolvency. The commissioners were supposed to collect debts owing to the bankrupt, and to distribute the proceeds among the creditors.[136] However, the 1571 statute gave little guidance as to what should be done when the bankrupt's debtor did not pay. There was no suggestion as to how the penalty on a bond could be executed. Power of assignment or transfer was not given to the commissioners. Yet in most instances it cannot have been desirable to give the bankrupt himself a free hand in recovering debts, and he was not supposed to have the money to pay lawyers and clerks. In 1604, the commissioners were authorized to assign bonds, debts, deeds, and recognizances so that their assignees, usually the bankrupt's creditors, could proceed in their own names.[137] The bankrupt's debtors were to be given due notice of the new state of affairs, and until this was done there was no bar against the bankrupt himself being repaid.[138] Creditors might use legal proceedings to enforce payment of debts, but money thus recovered, costs being deducted, was to be distributed.[139]

Measures such as those described above did little more than scratch the surface of accumulated legal rights and rules. In the reign of Charles II, some of the difficulties were summed up by Nottingham. When money was recovered by a Chancery decree, execution was not to be stayed even though the plaintiff was declared a bankrupt between decree and execution. On the other hand, money recovered by a Chancery decree for a man who was already declared to be a bankrupt could be assigned by the commissioners. The assignees were to have the benefit of recovery, and they could establish their right by exhibiting a bill in Chancery against the bankrupt and his debtor. This, Nottingham pointed out, was quite different from the situation at law where money recovered by a bankrupt could not be assigned before or after execution.[140]

A simple conclusion with respect to powers over

---

[129] 1604, *1.

[130] B. Montagu, *Some Observations upon the Bill for the Improvement of the Bankrupt Laws* (London, 1822), p. 8.

[131] 1624, *13.

[132] 1624, *10. However, it may be that, as Lord Hardwicke later asserted, this provision was not acted upon until 1736. Jenks, p. 277, n. 1.

[133] 1624, *11. The power to bar estates tail was a striking feature, and it apparently anticipated the plan adopted by the fines and recoveries act of 1833. Holdsworth **8**: p. 239, n. 5.

[134] 1624, *12. This was an uncertain authority both in terms of immediate law and the unresolved development of the equity of redemption. 1 Eq. Ca. Abr., 53. R. W. Turner, *The Equity of Redemption* (Cambridge, 1931), pp. 28, 55, 71–72, 82.

[135] 1571, *9, 10.

[136] 1571, *5.

[137] 1604, *8.

[138] 1604, *9. Nottingham, however, ruled that a voluntary payment to a bankrupt had to be paid again to the assignees of the commission. *Nottingham's Cases* **1**: p. 277. He admitted that no one could feel safe in paying a debt to a bankrupt or in receiving a debt from someone he knew to be a bankrupt. *Ibid.* **1**: p. 348. For a case where a creditor petitioned in Chancery for protection because he knew of a secret act of bankruptcy by his debtor, see *Nottingham's 'Prolegomena'*, p. 350. For the vexed question of damages recovered on a judgment clearly before the act of bankruptcy, see Cro. Car., 166, Benson v. Flower (1629).

[139] 1604, *7.

[140] *Nottingham's 'Manual'*, pp. 162–163.

property is that all these statutes were inadequate. The measures of 1604 and 1624 illustrated rather than solved problems which had been set in 1571. One more example may be given. The *quominus* fiction was based upon the fact or pretense that a creditor was indebted to the sovereign. In consequence, proceedings in the Exchequer were allowed. It would seem that commissioners were sometimes frustrated by creditors who secured an independent extent on this basis. In 1624, therefore, commissioners were empowered to inquire into the facts, and if fraud was present they were to convey or sell the debts or goods to the benefit of all the creditors. In theory this was a significant development, but in practice its utility may be doubted. The loopholes in statutory explanation were still there. What did the words *fraudulent* and *reputed* mean? How could an equity of redemption be utilized? These questions and others could only be decided by the courts.[141]

Problems of property, along with the determination of persons embraced by the statutes, represented areas in which there was great need for interpretation. Was there any significance, for example, in the fact that the Elizabethan act specifically mentioned copyholds whereas the two Jacobean ones did not? Quite properly, the judges decided that nothing need be read into this. In any case, it is apparent that the intention in 1604 and 1624 was to expand and not to repeal. However, as it was observed, the statutes "ought to be expounded liberally, and shall be construed accordingly, to make as strong provision as they may against the bankrupt." [142]

THE STATUS OF BANKRUPTCY COMMISSIONERS

Bankruptcy commissioners were sometimes accused of peculation, and their actions were occasionally said to be illegal and without authority.

Commissioners were most often critized for not attending meetings. The task, however, involved considerable expenditure of time: one commission held eighteen meetings between 22 November, 1622 and 1 October, 1623. Officials claimed to sit for hours, from 7:00 A.M until noon, or from 2 until 8:00 P.M, sometimes having to disperse for lack of a quorum.[143] Commissioners expected to be reimbursed for their personal expenses, but this was not mentioned in the statutes. It was, in consequence, easy to suggest that they had used the commission for their own gain, and the implication was reinforced in Charles I's reign once professional commissioners began to dominate.[144] Commissioners, it was said, "swallowed up as much of the poor bankrupt or pretended bankrupt his estate, by often and unnecessary sitting about the same. . . ." [145] Yet statutory guidance was not given.[146] The way was therefore open for proceedings in a variety of courts. Early in the reign of James I, Chancery gave relief to a "concealer" from whom too much had been taken "upon indirect dealing by commissioners." [147] In 1607 a group of commissioners, two of whom were possibly from Gray's Inn, were accused in Star Chamber of taking too much. The sums involved were small: two commissioners were said to have taken £5 and a third £12 in respect of riding charges and their pains. Coke said that judges, who got their fee from the crown, could not take other fees save in certain specified cases,[148] but these men were only commissioners. They were unsworn persons put in trust, and therefore they might take such fees as would reimburse them for their expenses.[149] He recognized, however, that it was difficult to draw lines of distinction, and said that "he was sorry they had taken anything." The court concurred with the tenor of Coke's remarks, and it was held that justifiable remuneration was proper. Lord Chancellor Ellesmere, however, disagreed with some of Coke's sentiments. Indeed he wished that the commissioners had taken more—"for with a lawyer *cessans lucrum damnum est*"—and he suggested that failure to receive adequate reimbursement for expenses would damage the competent execution of commissions.[150] The court fined some other persons who, claiming warrant from the commissioners of bankruptcy, had caused a riot by

---

141 1624, *9. There was uncertainty as to whether an act of bankruptcy committed in Ireland made a man bankrupt in England. *Nottingham's Cases* 2: p. 744. For this, and also whether those born in the Isle of Man could be bankrupts, see Goodinge, p. 34.

142 1571, *2. Cro. Car., 550, Crisp v. Pratt (1635). For copyholders, see also Cro. Car., 568–570, Parker v. Bleeke (1638). Goodinge, p. 97.

143 P.R.O., E215/3/232, 233, 234.

144 See above, p. 26.

145 Leach, *Proposals for an Act*, p. 17.

146 Nottingham acknowledged that commissioners should be reimbursed and that a case which involved frauds, concealments, and law-suits could legitimately create expenses which might erode the bankrupt's estate. However, he threw some light on improper practices when he said that expenses should not be allowed for meetings in taverns and for entertaining the commissioners. *Nottingham's 'Manual'*, pp. 164–165.

147 Tothill, 62, Wood v. Hayes (1606–1607).

148 For example, special assizes or error in London.

149 Coke was careful to point out that they must not contract a bargain beforehand for a reward or fee. An elaborate oath for commissioners of sewers was written into their controlling Statute (23 Henry VIII c. 5, *2) but bankruptcy commissioners were apparently only sworn from 1719, an oath being included in the 1732 statute. Holdsworth 1: p. 471. 5 George II c. 30, *43. Despite some evidence, I am not sure that there was anything to prevent the lord chancellor on his own authority from requiring bankruptcy commissioners to be sworn. In 1676, considering complaints of a creditor, Nottingham was at first unwilling to hear the case "because the commissioners were on their oaths, and if they did wrong were liable to an action at law . . . ." *Nottingham's Cases* 1: p. 313.

150 J. Hawarde, *Les Reportes del Cases in Camera Stellata*, ed. W. P. Baildon (London, 1894), pp. 342–343.

going with guns and other weapons to arrest the bankrupt during divine service on the sabbath.[151]

On 12 February, 1587, a group of creditors petitioned the lord chancellor after the alleged bankruptcy of John Cook. A commission was issued on 17 February. The sum claimed by the petitioning creditors was £271 1s. 0d. Four days later, the bankrupt conveyed goods worth £24 to Robert Tibnam, who was owed £64. Tibnam did not join in the commission, and his factor, Thomas Mills, refused to have anything to do with its proceedings. The commissioners, therefore, sold the assets to the other creditors, who subsequently brought an action. The question at issue was whether the sale by the commissioners was good despite the bankrupt's delivery of the same goods to Tibnam. Chief Justice Wray and his colleagues decided that the conveyance was valid. In explanation, it was said that the 1571 statute had been intended to secure an equal distribution among creditors, and that the bankrupt could not give preference to a single creditor at the expense of others. In any case, the bankrupt could not dispose of property after the award of a commission.

It would be unequal and unconscionable, and a great defect in the law, if after that he hath utterly discredited himself by becoming a bankrupt, the law should credit him to make distribution of his goods to whom he pleased, being a bankrupt man, and of no credit . . . . And the court resolved that the proviso concerning gifts and grants *bona fide*, makes no gift or grant good, which the bankrupt makes after he become bankrupt, but excludes them out of the penalty inflicted by the same proviso.

A creditor declining to join in the commission had forfeited his freedom of action until that commission had been wound up. The commission of bankruptcy itself was described as "matter of record" of which everyone must take notice.

This act gives benefit to those who will inquire and come in as creditors, and not to those, who either out of obstinacy refuse, or through carelessness neglect, to come before the commissioners, and pray the benefit of the said statute; for *vigilantibus et non dormientibus jura subveniunt,* for otherwise a debt might be concealed, or a creditor might absent himself, and so avoid all the proceedings of the commissioners by force of the said act. And every creditor may take notice of the commission, being matter of record, as is aforesaid, and so no inconvenience can happen to any creditor who will be vigilant; but great inconvenience will follow and the whole effect of the act be overthrown, if other construction should be made.[152]

Wray and his fellow judges had rejected the claims of a creditor who had tried to seek restitution outside the operations of a bankruptcy commission. There would be other cases and the commissioners, who worked by virtue of the 1571 and subsequent statutes, were not always to find their position so clearly maintained before the courts.

Seventeenth-century bankruptcy commissions have been described as the outstanding example of a judicial body, not possessing the attributes of a court of record, the decisions of which could be examined through collateral proceedings in the courts.[153] The commission had a statutory basis and the fact of its issue was supposedly a matter of record. The commissioners, however, did not constitute a court of record. At the beginning of the eighteenth century, Holt inferred that bankruptcy commissioners "had only an authority and not a jurisdiction." [154] Unlike commissions of sewers and justices of the peace, bankruptcy commissions were not apparently subject to writs of *certiorari*.[155] Indeed, insofar as this writ was used to transfer the record, with respect to bankruptcy commissions there was little to transfer. Even if the notion of "record"—which has its own meaning—is debased to that of documentation, there was only the original petition made to the chancellor and the possibility of some depositions and proceedings which could not in any case be read in Westminster Hall.[156] Even with the slow development of *certiorari* "to quash" after 1635, Miss Henderson has found no case before 1760 in which a *certiorari* actually was issued to a body which was clearly not a court of record.[157] The truth of the matter is that commissioners of bankruptcy were not judges, and they were appointed only in respect of the immediate case. At the most they were temporary and unsworn commissioners in whom was reposed a fiduciary trust. The point is clear from Coke.[158]

Certiorari was not applicable, but actions of tort lay to hand.[159] Commissioners could not expect protection if their decisions or acts were declared wrong in law. The 1604 statute tried to tackle the problem: if an action of trespass or any other suit was brought against the commissioners they were, by citing the authority of the two statutes, to plead the general issue and thus stand upon their statutory authority. If

[151] *Ibid.*, p. 343. Process could be served in church but an arrest could not be made.

[152] 2 Co. Rep. 25–26, The Case of Bankrupts (1589).

[153] Rubinstein, p. 60. Only in the nineteenth century was the so-called *Marshalsea* rule extended to bankruptcy commissions.

[154] Edith G. Henderson, *Foundations of English Administrative Law* (Cambridge, Mass., 1963), p. 114.

[155] *Ibid.*, pp. 28, 112.

[156] *Nottingham's Cases* 2: pp. 570–571.

[157] Henderson, p. 116.

[158] See above, p. 33.

[159] Rubinstein, p. 56. In 1666, it was pointed out that if the commissioners of bankruptcy decided contrary to law then the aggrieved party had his remedy by action. 2 Keble, 82, Bell v. Partridge. Holt, who could otherwise be misleading (see Henderson, p. 112), pointed out that "commissioners of bankrupts may commit a man for refusing to be examined concerning the estate of the bankrupt; but they are not judges; and their proceedings are traversable because their power of imprisonment is only *quousque*, etc." 1 Ld Ray., 467, De Groenvelt v. Burwell (1697).

the defendants, that is the commissioners, were upheld they were to receive costs.[160]

The actions of commissioners were constantly liable to challenge. In *Bonham's Case* it was said that the decision of commissioners that a man was a bankrupt could be traversed in an action of false imprisonment.[161] Hence, it is understandable that extreme caution in not overstepping the limits of authority became the rule. This was because collateral proceedings before the courts provided a form of supervision. Another form of supervision could be found in the general powers of the Privy Council, and in the indeterminate position of the lord chancellor, who alone had authority to issue a bankruptcy commission.

IV. PRIVY COUNCIL AND CHANCERY

Legislation provided narrow, and at times ambiguous, descriptions of persons liable to become bankrupt together with an outline of actions which constituted bankruptcy. Some people evaded bankruptcy because they did not behave in a specified fashion. Others were beyond the scope of bankruptcy procedures, whatever they did. Furthermore, the statutes required an initiative from creditors. These often saw no value in a state of bankruptcy being declared, possibly because they were willing to allow further time or even a composition. Hence all sorts of men were debtors, but only a tiny fraction could be bankrupts. It was along this sometimes fragile border between debt and bankruptcy that the Privy Council and the court of Chancery occasionally played a role of significance.

THE PRIVY COUNCIL AND DEBTORS

The situation of a debtor, dishonest or otherwise, was often fairly helpless unless he could persuade some agency to intervene on his behalf. The Privy Council naturally tried to aid enforcement of debt payments, but it also attempted to discourage or ameliorate imprisonment. One method was to secure an extension of time. This was particularly important since legal proceedings had the habit of escalating until the drain on the debtor's credit, which could also extend through to his sureties, reached disastrous proportions. A second method was to support or provide arbitration procedures after which, if the assets were not enough, a composition might be obtained.[1]

The absurdity of procedures in relation to debt was understood by many, but it was very difficult to find alternatives. In 1604, a bill to relieve prisoners in execution was turned down by the House of Commons. Only limited help could be expected from the statute of that year concerning small debts (those under forty shillings) and the relief of poor debtors in London.[2]

The Elizabethan Privy Council set up a series of commissions which were authorized to deal with the creditors of imprisoned debtors. One commission, specifically concerned with the King's Bench prison, was appointed in 1576 and was active for thirteen years. The commissioners were required to sit regularly, and a measure of their performance can be seen in the issue of commissions to handle the affairs of debtors in other prisons. The King's Bench commission was reorganized in 1589 and given authority to imprison for disobedience.[3]

The commissioners, notably those concerned with the King's Bench prison and the Fleet, were supposed to deal with creditors in the hope of securing a composition. However, their legal position was open to question, and they were sometimes sued in Common Pleas by virtue of informations on the statutes of *praemunire*. The Privy Council, in September, 1589, required the two chief justices, who had been made commissioners, to give advice when difficulties arose. It was also ordered that some commissioners should be ready to sit at least two days a week.[4]

Despite conundrums of jurisdiction, the late Elizabethan Council was ambitious in its attempts to help incarcerated debtors. In 1592, letters to the commissioners referred to complaints made by prisoners and noted some of the recognized problems. It was pointed out that many died in prison and that the creditors lost their money. Monthly meetings were to be held to hear "hard" cases, and creditors who would not come to heel were to be dealt with severely. The Privy Council appreciated the reluctance of commissioners to "constrain" creditors—it was admitted that their powers were insufficient—and advised that in cases of obstinacy the sitting commissioners should call upon "such other persons of quality and calling" as were named in the commission. In these and other circumstances, advice was to be sought from the two chief justices.[5] The shroud of legality was too doubtful, difficulties continued, and the mechanism was apparently abandoned for a time in the reign of James I. There were, of course, individual interventions, and commissions were set up for the King's Bench

[160] 1604, *11.

[161] 8 Co. Rep., 121a.

[1] J. P. Dawson, "The Privy Council and Private Law in the Tudor and Stuart Periods," *Michigan Law Review* **48** (1950) : pp. 411–413. Vincent Ponko, Jr., "The Privy Council and the Spirit of Elizabethan Economic Management," *Trans. Amer. Philos. Soc.* **58**, 4 (1968) : pp. 53–54.

[2] *CJ* 1: p. 290. In 1604 and 1606, statutes were passed which attempted to improve the situation for both creditors and debtors in London with respect to debts under forty shillings. 1 James I c. 14; 3 James I c. 15.

[3] Dawson, "Privy Council," pp. 415–416.

[4] *APC* 1581–1582, p. 175; 1587–1588, p. 99; 1589–1590, p. 109.

[5] *APC* 1591–1592, pp. 384–386.

prison and the Fleet in 1618.[6] Malynes thought that the commissioners had done a good job, and in 1622 he advocated their revival.[7] The 1624 statute crippled such approaches, but only if the debtor was capable of being a bankrupt. With respect to other debtors, the Council would make further attempts. In 1630, a commission empowered the archbishop of Canterbury, the bishop of London, the lord mayor of London, and others to compound with the creditors of prisoners when the debt was less than £200. Prisoners soon claimed that nothing was achieved. The problem was nationwide: the palatine Chancery at Durham issued commissions in 1638 and 1640 because of the numbers of imprisoned small debtors without means of repayment. "Most of the creditors are very unmerciful so as the poor prisoners are like to die and end their days there." [8]

It was only natural that intervention in favor of imprisoned debtors should raise difficulties. When possible, it was much easier for the Council to act at an earlier stage, and some debtors were not slow to seek help. Certainly the Council always appeared ready to influence creditors who stood out against a suggested composition—either in terms of time or in other ways—especially when it seemed that the debtor would meet his obligations if allowed liberty.[9] It might appoint a commission to treat with the creditors and to report back if any refused to cooperate. In this eventuality, the point was made that further action could be taken for the debtor's relief in equity and conscience.[10] Creditors, it must be remembered, would wish to be spared the cost and delay of litigation and debtors had many possibilities open to them. However, the cases that catch the eye tend to be those which center upon reluctant creditors.

On one occasion, the Council commissioned the lord mayor, sheriffs, and aldermen of London to meet with a set of creditors, "especially such as will be most rigorous." Their task, after suitable inquiries, was to secure time for the debtor to recover his own goods which were scattered in the houses of other persons. In the meantime, at least until discussions with the creditors had been completed, the sheriffs and the secondaries of both compters were to see that no arrest, action, or attachment was made against the debtor.[11] The Council would even authorize a commission of merchants to inquire specifically into the claims, reimbursement, and attitudes of creditors.[12] Thus in 1614, it helped a clothier of Cranbrooke who had, according to his own statement, given too much credit to people who subsequently went bankrupt, and who was now ready to accept almost any settlement, preferably a composition, if only he could get time to repair his estate. The creditors of a bankrupt were often on the verge of that state themselves.[13]

Malynes gave strong approval to the system whereby licenses from merchants, a traditional procedure, were given to debtors so that they could continue in business and thus enhance the possibility of a speedy settlement.[14] Creditors who had been soothed by Privy Council intervention might well provide their debtor with a license. Otherwise the Council could solicit or order some such grant. There were also letters of protection granted by the sovereign, commonly through the lord chancellor. These were normally issued to persons who had to go abroad or were engaged in government business, and therefore unable to attend to their personal affairs.[15]

Various forms of license and protection were always available. They were either a fact with which the Privy Council had to deal or an allowance sponsored by it. With or without an original petition from the creditors, the Council might endeavor to ensure through commissioners that a commercial debtor was allowed to "pass with free liberty" in order to recover debts, and it would protect him from writs, arrests, and executions.[16] In the reign of James I an important grocer, Andrew Palmer, delivered all his effects to his creditors and undertook to pay all his debts over further time in return for "a letter of license under their hands." This expired before everything had been repaid, but the Privy Council came to Palmer's help after he had been thrown into Canterbury prison by three creditors, and again when subsequently he was in the King's Bench prison.[17] In the 1570's, the Council supported a debtor who had obtained a letter of protection and who promised that the principal would be repaid with ten per cent profit if he and his surety were left alone. This seemed to be an

[6] Dawson, "Privy Council," p. 416.

[7] Malynes, *Lex Mercatoria*, p. 157. William Leach also advocated a system of commissions, albeit of a different nature, for the mutual relief of creditors and poor prisoners. *Proposals for an Act for Speedy Settling at Large all Prisoners, both for Damages and Debt* (London, 1649).

[8] *D.K.Rep.* App., Privy Seals, Signet Bills, etc., 1625–1632, p. 173. P.R.O., Durham 4/1, pp. 572, 573. *CSP Dom.* 1629–1631, p. 370. For debates and proposals during the Commonwealth as to imprisoned debtors, see Veall, pp. 142–151.

[9] *APC* 1613–1614, pp. 102–103, 169–170, 472, 522–523. See *CSP Dom.* 1633–1634, pp. 307–308; 1637, p. 239.

[10] *APC* 1590, p. 98.

[11] *APC* 1581–1582, pp. 112–113.

[12] *APC* 1577–1578, p. 71. The debtor was listed as being a bankrupt.

[13] *APC* 1613–1614, p. 472. In 1576, the Council aided a creditor serving in Ireland whose debtors refused to come to a composition. *APC* 1575–1577, pp. 212–213. For some difficulties of a merchant moneylender in securing repayment from great clients, see A. H. Dodd, "Mr. Myddelton, the Merchant of Tower Street," *Elizabethan Government and Society*, ed. S. T. Bindoff, J. Hurstfield, C. Williams (London, 1961), p. 262.

[14] Malynes, *Lex Mercatoria*, p. 157.

[15] Jones, *Chancery*, pp. 204–206.

[16] *APC* 1587–1588, pp. 16–17.

[17] *APC* 1616–1617, pp. 120–121, 190.

instance where a man with essentially good credit had been placed under impossible pressure. Commissioners, in this case men of such high standing as the lord mayor and the master of the rolls, were required to achieve such an accord, but it was stipulated that the letter of protection must be surrendered.[18] The Elizabethan Council also seems to have endorsed, at least tacitly, the position of foreign merchants who preferred traditional ways. When an Italian was unable to meet his debts, the Council wrote to the master of the rolls and the solicitor general in support of the merchant's request for a year's freedom from arrest and molestation by his creditors. This was to be "upon some reasonable order by them or other indifferent person to be made between them." [19]

Examples could be multiplied, although one must be careful not to exaggerate the extent of Privy Council activity. Affairs of debt noted in the register are few. There is, however, one exceptional story which spans the central period of Elizabeth's reign. This concerns a merchant who does not appear to have gone bankrupt. His plight, and his ability to manipulate Privy Council support, does much to illustrate the approach of that body towards debtors from the mercantile community.

WILLIAM NUTSHAWE

The story of William Nutshawe, merchant of Southampton, was set against a background provided by broad considerations of foreign policy and England's varying relations with France. In general, English merchants enjoyed favorable conditions under the Treaty of Blois, arranged by Charles IX in 1572 and confirmed by Henry III in 1575. The effect of this was disrupted but not entirely destroyed by the later civil wars. On the grounds of breach in continuity, however, Henry IV would not recognize the treaty.[20]

In Nutshawe's case, diplomatic circumstances encouraged the Privy Council to provide support because his troubles did not stem from dishonesty. On the other hand, there must have been some question as to how far his misfortune resulted from rash behavior. The Council seems to have given him the benefit of the doubt, but the venture which drew him into trouble was something of a gamble.

This saga began in the late 1560's when a consignment of wheat sent to La Rochelle was captured by the French royal forces. Nutshawe had bills for his consignment and expected repayment, but the official French position, while it would fluctuate, was that the cargo was good prize since it had been intended for the king's enemies. This was the substance of one judgment eventually delivered by the French Council.[21]

By October, 1573, when Lord Treasurer Burghley and other ministers were preoccupied with marriage negotiations, the English representative in Paris, Dr. Valentine Dale, was pursuing the matter. Some months later, he reported that there was a reasonable hope of the claim being settled. Dale was confident. He sent Nutshawe, who had come over in attendance of his suit, home "with good and evident testimony of his rights and of the diligence of them both." It was, nonetheless, confessed that the attitude of the French government left much to be desired. A warrant for repayment had been granted to Nutshawe, but it "was directed to such men as either say they have no money, or that they have nothing to do with the matter, or dwell as far as Marseilles and in the Island of Rhé, and such other places as are more than dangerous to come by." The death of Charles IX threatened to blight even this devious progress, but Dale's dispatches continued to be optimistic. He reported that restitution for wrongs done to English merchants had been ordered and that satisfaction for Nutshawe figured prominently in this command. It was a forlorn expectation. The argument dragged on, and it assumed enough significance to appear first among the items on Lord North's "Private Memorial" when he arrived in Paris on a special embassy. North, a Leicester supporter, was not inclined to aid pacific arrangements between the two countries. At any rate Dale, who was Burghley's man, was ready to drop the matter. Nonetheless, it was kept alive by occasional intimations of a settlement.[22]

Meanwhile, Nutshawe's creditors at home were impatient. On 12 July, 1575, the Privy Council requested them to forbear for six months so that he could again visit France in order to prosecute his suit. Two days later, his favorable standing with the Council was emphasized when the commissioners in restraint of grain for Dorset were ordered to permit him to buy and export two hundred quarters, "if the same may be conveniently spared without enhancing the prices of the markets." [23] Not long after, following assurances from Henry III and his ambassador in London, de la Mothe Fénélon, the Privy Council again required Nutshawe's creditors to forbear for six months, "by which time he may be either paid in France, or her Majesty upon denial of justice is to take other order for him and other her subjects in like suit." [24]

[18] *APC* 1571–1575, p. 128.
[19] *APC* 1577–1578, p. 403.
[20] Beatrice Reynolds, "Elizabethan Traders in Normandy," *Jour. Mod. Hist.* 9 (1937) pp. 289–303. See generally R. B. Wernham, *Before the Armada* (London, 1966) and C. Read, *Lord Burghley and Queen Elizabeth* (New York, 1960).
[21] *CSP For.* 1585–1586, p. 245.
[22] *CSP For.* 1572–1574, pp. 433, 467, 471, 507, 533, 563, 570–571.
[23] *APC* 1575–1577, pp. 5–6.
[24] *APC* 1575–1577, pp. 78–79.

Promises rather than outright failure were the product of the next two years. Dale grew tired of the rigmarole whereby he was balked by protestations of settlement, which he had to accept with as good grace as he could muster. "These doings," he wrote to Burghley, "will make a man *Didymus* in all things." After a particularly irritating passage—as humorous as it was absurd—he remarked, "God help them that have to do in this court." Nutshawe had actually been given warrants for repayment, but no day was specified. The French treasurer would not be drawn into naming a time for satisfaction, but he tried to extract an absolute acquittance from Nutshawe. This move was roundly dismissed by Dale as a trick, and he subsequently reported that the warrants were anyhow on money owing to the French crown. They were directed to the treasurer of the Espargne, but this official maintained that they could only be paid out of a debt due to the king at Angers. Messengers were sent but, or so it was asserted, they were attacked and robbed, and one of their companions slain. In any case, the debtors of the French crown refused to pay up. This, Dale was told, was because "they cannot enjoy the bargain for the which they should pay their money, by reason of a former bargain made by the King unto another." Yet Nutshawe could only be paid through this source. Described as wearied, discouraged, and burdened with debt, he left Paris.[25]

In July, 1576, the Privy Council was again asking Nutshawe's creditors to forbear. Dale reported in August, however, that the money was at last available. The treasurer of the Espargne wanted an acquittance, but Dale insisted that this could be given in England to the French ambassador or to a man whose goods were stayed at Nutshawe's suit. Nothing happened, but this hint from the French authorities may have been prompted by Nutshawe's search for other forms of remuneration. He obtained an order from the court of Admiralty for stay of certain sums in the hands of London merchants, "appertaining by way of assurance to some merchants of Paris."[26] Nutshawe, together with a ship and goods, was arrested in April, 1578, on complaint that the vessel was a French one taken by him in an act of piracy two years previously. He replied that the ship had been in his possession for ten years, and in a counter accusation stated that he himself had been the victim of French pirates.[27] The Privy Council again protected him on 24 August, 1578. This time he was awarded an eight-month barrier against molestation of his person, goods, and sureties.[28] It transpired that he had appropriated a ship of Marshal de Biron. This may have been a castaway. There were other French complaints, some of which were probably unjustified, but the Privy Council ordered the captain of the Isle of Wight to impound one of Nutshawe's ships, "The Barque of Boulogne."[29] Yet on 28 June, 1579, the Council required his creditors to forbear for another ten months, and in justification they cited his great losses, the arrest of his goods in France, and his deprivations at sea.[30]

The Privy Council was willing to go to remarkable lengths to protect Nutshawe and to improve his position. In May, 1580, he was given a license to export three hundred quarters of grain from Norfolk. Councillors must have been aware that their attitude was exceptional. Two months earlier, in stipulating another three-months forbearance, the language of the Council was less direct and more apologetic than on previous occasions. Instead of issuing a command, it was indicated that the Council would "take in good part" the creditors adopting an attitude of restraint.[31]

The affair dragged on during the 1580's. French intransigence was matched by Nutshawe's ability to take reprisal against French goods in England. It was asserted that his exploits on the seas had led to the seizure of property worth over forty thousand crowns in less than four months, "and some of the poor people have died of despair." It is surprising, therefore, to find that Mauvissière, French ambassador in England from 1575 to 1585, transmitted over £880 early in 1585. In fact the ambassador, by his own account, had acted prematurely and without proper authority. He was sharply reminded by his superiors that the grain in dispute had been consigned to La Rochelle in contravention of the commands and interests of the king of France. The French government, possibly in reaction to Nutshawe's recent activities but also because of the changed mood in Paris, was no longer willing to talk about repayment. It had reverted to the position that nothing was due. Mauvissière professed to have acted on the request of Henry III that he do his best to maintain good relations with Queen Elizabeth and her subjects. For this error in interpretation he was called before the French Council, where, as he sadly told Walsingham, he tried to show that Nutshawe had been paid by the king's order: "which they would not believe." Mauvissière must have regretted his "simplicity urged on by a desire to do good."[32] The French ambassador may have made a mistake, but perhaps unwittingly he relieved the Privy Council from further responsibility. At any rate Nutshawe's wife, in an appeal to the Coun-

[25] *CSP For.* 1575–1577, pp. 88, 125, 154, 173–174, 178, 203, 213, 237, 238, 252, 278–279, 316.

[26] *APC* 1575–1577, pp. 154, 174. *CSP For.* 1575–1577, p. 365.

[27] *CSP For.* 1577–1578, p. 634; 1579–1580, p. 14.

[28] *APC* 1577–1578, p. 315.

[29] *APC* 1578–1580, pp. 36, 99, 105, 259. The ship was eventually bargained for by a gentleman follower of the Duke of Anjou.

[30] *APC* 1578–1580, p. 171.

[31] *APC* 1578–1580, pp. 427–428; 1580–1581, p. 7.

[32] *CSP For.* 1584–1585, p. 547; 1585–1586, p. 245.

cil, subsequently deplored the severity of her husband's creditors.[33]

For the better part of two decades, the Privy Council had protected Nutshawe. His initial circumstances were not greatly different from those of other debtors who were actually declared to be bankrupt. During this period, however, he had not apparently committed an act recognized by the bankruptcy statutes, or at least one which allowed the effective operation of bankruptcy commissioners. Had he been careless about obtaining official sanction for his journeys abroad, or if he had stayed too long in his house (possibly due to illness) the way might have been open for bankruptcy proceedings, assuming that this was desired by a sufficient number of creditors. This exceptional story is important because it illustrates the fine line which separated bankruptcy from general situations of debt or insolvency.

THE PRIVY COUNCIL AND BANKRUPTS

The Privy Council occasionally intervened in the conduct of bankruptcy proceedings. Warning letters were sent to some commissioners who were suspected of being laggards,[34] and the lord chancellor was notified when it was reported that nothing was being done.[35] Once, in 1619, it was doubted if there were grounds for a commission of bankruptcy which had been issued. Debts due had been paid, other debts were not yet due, and the debtor had not absented himself. Hence the Council appointed its own commission with instructions to mediate outstanding difficulties and report obstinate creditors.[36] A somewhat similar situation occurred in the reign of Elizabeth after a bankruptcy commission had been sued out by some foreign merchants, presumably under the 1543 statute. The commissioners and creditors had then agreed to give further time, since the debtor appeared to be capable of meeting his obligations. Bonds were entered for this curious composition, but the debtor subsequently claimed to have acted under duress.[37] On another occasion, the Council was asked to consider a man who had conveyed his possessions to his son-in-law, and then "shifted himself out of the way, and become voluntarily in quality of a bankrupt," leaving his sureties to carry the burden.[38]

Most interventions by the Privy Council can be described as incidental. When Anthony Tuck, a merchant of Rouen, went broke in that town, the Council ordered the lord mayor of London to arrange his arrest and to have him kept in the house of some honest merchant. His goods in England were impounded towards the satisfaction of his English creditors, but London authorities directed the surplus to be used in meeting a debt of £65 owed to a French creditor.[39] Late in 1591, during a vacancy in the lord chancellorship, there was hesitation over a petition for a bankruptcy commission; the Council asked the lord mayor and the wardens of the haberdashers "to take order" with the debtor for satisfaction of what was owing or else certify "whether you shall find him to be bankrupt." [40]

The Council sometimes tried to obtain forbearance by arguing that delay might be more beneficial to all concerned than a partitition of available assets. In 1619, it acted over the head of a bankruptcy commission, but on this occasion the problem was one of public concern. Many clothiers, few of whom were noticeably wealthy, obtained wool from the farmer on a credit basis, paying for it when the cloths had been disposed of by the merchant. If the merchant's credit collapsed, the repercussions would spread back to shatter both clothier and farmer. This had happened in the particular case. The bankrupt merchant, who owed £20,000 to eighty clothiers in Essex and Suffolk, had conveyed his property to others. Unemployment was feared, and the Council had reason to suppose that its own commission, which included the master of the rolls and Sir Edward Coke, might be preferable to proceedings under the bankrupty statutes.[41]

The good offices of the Council were sometimes solicited by creditors outside the commission. The rule of rate and rate alike, to the exclusion of those outside, was sometimes improper or unfair. In January, 1582, shortly after Philip II had taken over Portugal, it was ordered that the ambassador of the late king of Portugal, who was owed £100 by a bankrupt, was to be paid in full, since he had come to England as representative of a living king "and is not as yet but to be esteemed as a public person." [42] In another case, the bankruptcy commission had made a distribution, the two bankrupts had died, and the petitioner who was owed £100 could not get aything, although £80 was left. The actual decision was left to the lord keeper, but the Council suggested that any surplus

[33] P.R.O., S.P.12/235, no. 91. He is described as "late" of Southampton.

[34] *APC* 1580–1581, pp. 341–342.

[35] *APC* 1629–1630, pp. 391–393.

[36] *APC* 1619–1621, p. 32.

[37] *APC* 1586–1587, pp. 95–96.

[38] *APC* 1586–1587, pp. 78–79.

[39] *APC* 1571–1575, pp. 301, 375. This was well within the power of the city authorities if the creditors were citizens of London, but in this instance evidently some or all did not have this status. It may be noted that in the early seventeenth century Chancery assisted foreign creditors when an Englishman, resident abroad, transferred his property and person to England. Tothill, 68–69, Monro, pp. 167–169, Seve v. Colly (1610–1612).

[40] *APC* 1591–1592, p. 130.

[41] *APC* 1619–1621, pp. 79–80. J. E. Pilgrim, "The Cloth Industry in Essex and Suffolk, 1558–1640," unpub. London M.A. thesis (1938), p. 165.

[42] *APC* 1581–1582, pp. 310–311.

might as well be paid to this man.[43] A more interesting case concerned the sale of kerseys worth £40 to a merchant just prior to his bankruptcy. The vendors wanted the kerseys returned, since their retention by the commissioners would enforce sharing in bankruptcy proceedings, with the distinct possibility that only a percentage would be recovered. Although the rules prevented special consideration after the issue of a bankruptcy commission, the Council wrote to the Earl of Pembroke, asking him to deal in equity and conscience in the matter.[44]

Not too much should be made of the scattered handful of bankruptcy situations tackled by the Privy Council. Even so, its position and freedom of initiative were severely damaged by the 1624 statute. This struck against those who by petition or bill tried to get their creditors to accept less than was due or to secure a longer day of repayment than was allowed in the original agreement.[45] The Council's former interest in prisoners had for the time been shattered, and its general position with respect to debtors had been undermined. Seeking a protection could henceforth be construed as an act of bankruptcy if the statutes applied. However, the possibility of Council intervention in bankruptcy proceedings was not totally destroyed. It continued to be involved with debtors, possibly on a reduced scale, and occasionally it acted on petitions complaining about the handling of bankruptcy matters.[46]

After 1624, nonetheless, approaches by a debtor to the Council could result in his being declared a bankrupt, if his occupation was embraced by the relevant statutes. In theory, a minority of creditors could petition for a bankruptcy commission if the majority, using the good offices of the Council, were willing to agree to extra time or even accept a composition for the total sum due. However, there were still circumstances in which the Council might act. In one case, it was supposed that those owing money to a debtor had withheld payment for fear that they might "be forced to pay over again upon a commission of bankrupts." This was in 1637, and the Council did "not hold it reasonable that the commissions of bankrupts should be used to uphold and strengthen the willfulness of a few against the general and charitable consent of the greatest number of creditors." Lord Keeper Coventrye agreed with this sentiment, and he promised to ensure that a commission was not issued at the behest of creditors who had refused a composition. The Council was going against the tide of parliamentary sentiment expressed in 1621, but it was by no means clear that Coventrye had the power to refuse a commission. Nottingham later decided that this option did not exist.[47] In the late 1630's however, it looks as though the Council was being more assertive and trying to escape from a situation in which its role had been circumscribed. The possibilities cannot be assessed because the immediate future lay with Long Parliament, Civil Wars, and Interregnum.

THE LORD CHANCELLOR AND THE COURT OF CHANCERY

The courts of law and their records obviously provide a fuller background to the affairs of men who might become bankrupt than is true of the occasional activity of the Privy Council. Most important was the position of the lord chancellor and the court of Chancery.

The jurisdiction of the court of Chancery cannot be defined in terms of economic or social convenience. It handled litigation of commercial or industrial content on grounds which were far removed from any claim to supervise the business and trading community. The historian searching for evidence of international mercantile transactions should turn first to the records of the High Court of Admiralty. Nonetheless, Chancery records are rich in information about contracts, credit methods, and the debts of merchants and tradesmen. Particular note may be taken of the bill of exchange which Chancery, apparently to a lesser degree than the Admiralty, was prepared to recognize as a valid contract. By this means, a man who owed money could empower a creditor abroad to recover from a debtor who was also abroad. It was common to assign bills of exchange, and so they served as "a 'traveller's cheque' as much as a way of paying debts." [48] The bill of exchange was not fully negotiable, but Chancery acknowledged its validity just as it recognized most technicalities surrounding situations of debt and contract. This meant that it often had to find out the relevant customs and practices of merchants or discover the proper form and conditions of such an instrument.[49] Chancery would play some part in bringing about a common form for bills of exchange and hasten their recognition at common law.[50] Bankruptcy, in contrast, was a statutory creation surrounded by complications both novel and traditional. As in the general area of debt, the Chan-

[43] *APC* 1577–1578, p. 15.

[44] *APC* 1577–1578, pp. 37, 66.

[45] 1624, *2.

[46] *Privy Council Registers* 1637–1645, 2: p. 410; 3: pp. 36–37.

[47] *CSP Dom.* 1636–1637, p. 351. See below, p. 49.

[48] Harding, pp. 318–319.

[49] One case resulted in an order for repayment of a debt of £72 lent by bill of exchange for dealings in broadcloths and kerseys. P.R.O., C.33/81, ff. 21v–22, Pinsowld v. Puliston (1590). It appears that a person who accepted a bill of exchange was not liable to pay on it unless he was challenged within three days after the sum was due. P.R.O., C.24/100, Whit v. Lenarte (1571).

[50] Most generalizations are open to question until more records have been studied. Chancery probably had an advan-

cery bench would discover that attempts to arrange compositions or encourage restraint (both being normal mercantile practices) would, in the reign of James I, raise a tide of opposition which could not be resisted.

The court of Chancery, which embraced both an equitable and a common law jurisdiction, was very much the court of the lord chancellor. It is often necessary, therefore, to draw a distinction between the jurisdiction of the lord chancellor and that of his court, because he exercised powers, sometimes bestowed by statute, which related to his position as a great officer of state rather than to his status as the judge of Chancery. Examples can be seen in affairs of marine insurance, charitable uses, and his traditional role as protector of infants and lunatics. Sometimes these powers expired. Others endured, and since it was only natural for the chancellor to utilize the facilities and process of Chancery his particular responsibility might merge with the general jurisdiction of the court. We are thus dealing with a distinction which was sometimes tenuous and temporary. The lord chancellor, for example, had authority to issue a *ne exeat regnum* to prevent an individual from going abroad, but motions to obtain or quash this writ could result in debate before the Chancery bench. The matter was so important (it was used against "great bankrupts, in whose estate many subjects are interested") that rules concerning the issue of this process were included in the general orders of the court.[51]

Nonetheless, distinctions between chancellor and Chancery were valid. The early bankruptcy statutes gave certain powers and responsibilities to the lord chancellor without reference to the court of Chancery. Faced by a fairly chaotic conflict of facts, interpretations, and jurisdictional doubts, Nottingham in the later seventeenth century produced an interpretation of the situation as it had developed since 1571. He illustrated that the state of affairs was seriously at fault, and then implemented as far as possible his own proposals for improving the authority of the lord chancellor.[52]

Although the lord chancellor was only one among several dignitaries mentioned by the Henrician statute, he was the most obvious official to be included in a petition. In practice, this meant that the clerical services of Chancery would be called upon. In the early years of Elizabeth's reign, Lord Keeper Bacon sometimes appointed a commission orally from the Chancery bench. The details were entered into the books kept by the register of the court. Once this was done, it was logical to utilize Chancery process against recalcitrants, whether these were bankrupts, creditors, or commissioners. Indeed instructions were sometimes given that commissioners should refer to the court if difficulties occurred.[53] This possibility was particularly valuable to creditors seeking protection from subsequent suits aimed at recovering a bankrupt's effects. A Chancery injunction was awarded against the administrator of a bankrupt who had commenced action at law for recovery of the goods distributed by the commission.[54]

While there do not seem to have been many cases, a Chancery jurisdiction over bankruptcy, as defined by the 1543 statute, was apparently developing prior to 1571. This may be why the 1571 statute gave sole authority for the issue of commissions to the lord chancellor. However, this Elizabethan legislation was sufficiently precise to make the development of a regular Chancery jurisdiction well-nigh impossible, while being too imprecise to allow of any adequate alternative. Even so, Chancery was still the most obvious court to be used as an ancillary to bankruptcy proceedings: it could compel a sworn taking of accounts,[55] and it could probably enforce discovery against a bankrupt and others.[56] Decades later, Nottingham said that the particular value of Chancery proceedings was that all the parties could be brought before the court.[57] However, these and other powers did not imply an automatic or special relationship. Chancery was used in this way to aid proceedings before all kinds of courts and tribunals, lay and ecclesiastical, civil and criminal, royal and manorial.

The general nature of Chancery's jurisdiction was

---

tage because of its ability to make a simple order for payment. Courts following a common law procedure were more circumscribed, but something could be done to achieve the same end through *assumpsit*, and in 1666 acceptance was obtained of an action on the case upon the custom of merchants. Harding, p. 319. For the employment of bills of exchange with respect to inland transactions in the mid-seventeeth century, and resulting common law complexities, see J. K. Horsefield, *British Monetary Experiments, 1650–1710* (London, 1960), pp. xii–xiii. For bills of exchange in general and other matters, see J. Milnes Holden, *The History of Negotiable Instruments in English Law* (London, 1955).

51 Sanders 1, i: pp. 120–121. Jones, *Chancery*, p. 204.

52 Nottingham's major reflections are in the *'Manual'*, pp. 161–165. See below, pp. 40–41. Some subsequent developments can be seen from 1 Eq. Ca. Abr., 52–56.

53 P.R.O., C.33/27, ff. 105, 262v., 270v., Frenche *et alii, quer.*, Frycand v. Calverly, and Spinola v. Mere (1562); C.33/29, f. 340, Berde *et alii, quer.* (1564).

54 P.R.O., C.33/31, f. 90v., Austen v. Bawe (1565).

55 In October, 1614, Ellesmere indicated that Chancery's ability to examine accounts on oath was severely limited unless covin and fraud were suspected. Sanders 1, i: p. 86.

56 See *Nottingham's Cases* 1: pp. cxvii, 221. One defendant, a scrivener, demurred. He argued that the information was privileged and that the confidence reposed in him should be respected as would be that between a lawyer and his client. Nottingham, however, said that a scrivener, far from being a "civil confessor as a lawyer is," was "a person suspected in law as apt to make unlawful concealments." *Ibid.* 2: pp. 498–499. For discovery against a creditor, see *ibid.* 2: pp. 554–555.

57 *Nottingham's 'Manual'*, pp. 162–163.

sufficient to ensure that the court sometimes played a supervisory role. Granted that someone exhibited a bill of complaint, the court could oversee the proceedings of commissioners in selling the goods and lands of bankrupts, and it could try to ensure that all the creditors benefited equally.[58] One group of commissioners, having impounded the assets, was dubious whether an act of bankruptcy had in fact occurred. Debts were nonetheless owed, and Chancery in effect influenced the commission towards making a composition.[59] This court had no claim of jurisdiction over title to real property, but it could be of assistance in sorting out tricky questions surrounding the ownership of personal property when, for example, the rights of third parties were involved. In the middle of Elizabeth's reign, Nicholas Stockbridge bought goods at Antwerp from Danyell Rantflesh and promised to deliver kerseys in repayment on the next arrival of ships from London. Stockbridge paid the customs at London. The goods were then handed over to Thomas Speart, who almost immediately went bankrupt. Chancery decided that some items belonged to Stockbridge, and that they ought not to be handed over to Speart's creditors. The interesting factor is the procedure adopted. Petitioned by Rantflesh and others, the court had referred the matter to the bankruptcy commissioners. The latter, in reporting the proper course to take, acted more in accordance with authority given by Chancery than that provided by their commission.[60] The point has been seen before. It was wrong to force a man into being a creditor when his goods could be returned. Otherwise, intending bankrupts could manipulate the situation, and there was always the possibility of securing a composition or more favorable arrangements under the continuing cloak of a bankruptcy commission. Thomas Speart, for example, had previously been bankrupt and was probably a shrewd operator. His former creditors, some "poor" clothiers in the north of England, had discovered that his assets hardly covered one-third of his debts.[61]

A late Elizabethan case underlines the kind of problem posed by those who deliberately courted bankruptcy. John de Boys, a merchant stranger, handed over some brass to an English creditor, Coolye. This was partly to satisfy the debt and partly in return for cloth. He undertook to pay for all cloth received above the value of the brass. De Boys was making similar arrangements with other creditors, and so Coolye delivered only enough cloth to cover the value of the brass. De Boys, however, was "playing bankrupt." He made a "colorable" deed of gift to some other merchants, and these claimed that Coolye should fulfill his bargain and deliver all the cloth. This would have compelled him to become a joint creditor and only receive a rate for what he was owed. He, therefore, initiated proceedings in Chancery. The recommendation of a master was that the contract should be voided, since Coolye would otherwise be stampeded into the position of becoming a creditor after the declaration of bankruptcy.[62]

Depositions in another late Elizabethan case illustrate the information which may be culled from Chancery proceedings. Robert Nicholson, a London merchant, went bankrupt and was imprisoned. The exact circumstances of this confinement are not clear. However, he had consigned much of his estate to a single creditor, and the Chancery suit apparently represented an attempt by other creditors to overturn a *fait accompli* against which the bankruptcy commission, armed only with the authority provided in 1571, was nearly powerless. Witnesses examined in Chancery revealed that Nicholson's house in the Poultry had contained plate and household stuff worth £200, twenty-two packs of flax worth £400, and other commodities including buckram, wool, and Hampshire kerseys. Corn, cattle, and household items were at another house in Bramley, Surrey. Nicholson also had valuable interests overseas. His factor in Elburg, a London vintner, said that Nicholson "when he brake" had property worth twelve thousand florins (£2,400) in money, bills, and goods: alum, gilt leather, iron, amber, flax, hemp, canvas, linen cloth, and other fabrics. Most of this had been assigned to the principal creditor in a transaction which required the factor to work for the new owner, in return for which "his salary and pains should be satisfied to his contentment." The debtor was subtle. He had committed his supposed act of bankruptcy on 12 February, 1600, but official news of this would have taken some time to reach Elburg. In the meantime, the factor had been ordered to supervise a transference of assets to the principal creditor and his agents. This conveyance was made on 4 April. One of the conditions was that goods bought for Nicholson, whether before or after this date, should also be conveyed. This Chancery case, therefore, seems to involve the position of an individual creditor and the status of after-acquired property, consideration of which was com-

---

[58] P.R.O., C.33/81, f. 71: C.38/83, f. 22v. The lord chancellor could stand on both sides of the divide. In the reign of Elizabeth, Bromley authorized a commission to settle the debts of Anthony Marley, partner in an ironfounding enterprise at Merthyr, who was in danger of going bankrupt. In fact he seems to have done so, and Bromley's successor, Hatton, was involved in attempts to enforce settlement of the bankruptcy commission's arrangements. J. W. Gough, *The Rise of the Entrepreneur* (London, 1969), p. 83.

[59] P.R.O., C.33/103, f. 35, Bird v. Gamersall (1602). The case is possibly related to the one noted below, n. 63.

[60] P.R.O., C.38/1, Rantflesh v. Barneham (1582).

[61] *CSP Dom.* 1547–1580, p. 569.

[62] P.R.O., C.38/2, Coolye v. Victor (1597).

plicated by the fact that the goods in question were purchased abroad.[63]

Sloppy work by commissioners could also involve Chancery and other courts. This was most likely when insufficient attention was paid to the fact that a commission had to work not in a vacuum but amid a host of legal rights. *Allen's Case*, which lasted for over a decade and helped to raise fundamental questions as to Chancery jurisdiction, is a classic example.[64]

The story began with a merchant and former sheriff of York who went bankrupt in 1603 on being outlawed for debt. The bankruptcy commission sold his lands, said to be worth £2,400, to Allen and another creditor for £400. This was because the property was saddled with encumbrances made before the bankrupt had become indebted to any of the petitioners who had solicited the commission. However, it was stipulated that if this property was resold for a greater sum within three years, the profit was to be shared among all the creditors. Subsequently, in 1606, the commissioners arranged a composition for all the debts to be paid at the rate of ten shillings in the pound. This agreement was coupled with a bargain and sale of the lands to two other creditors at their real value. These two, one of whom had not initially joined in the bankruptcy proceedings, undertook to pay off the debts and encumbrances. Allen and his friend rejected this arrangement. They claimed that the encumbrances, essentially the debts due to others, were fraudulent, and they initiated proceedings in Chancery. It was quite proper to sue in Chancery if there was a doubt about the encumbrances, and it must also be said that the commissioners had rather complicated the situation. The two other creditors joined with the bankrupt in a cross bill calling for performance of the composition arranged by the commissioners and conveyance of the land. The resulting decree was in favor of Allen and his associate. They were to keep the lands, paying the remaining £30 due on a mortgage, and other encumbrances including a statute for £2,000 were discharged. Proceedings of execution upon a remaining statute of £1,500 were subsequently stayed. All this had taken some time, but the basic point was that within the three years originally specified the bankruptcy commissioners had found purchasers willing to pay the real value of the lands and to assume responsibility for payment of debts under the composition. Allen and his friend, if they intended to keep the lands as allowed by Chancery, should therefore have paid over the difference. This they declined to do.

There were many complications and characters involved at this stage, not least Allen's seizure of beasts belonging to the bankrupt's father and resulting actions in the King's Bench. The positions of the commissioners and Chancery were reconcilable, but both were concentrating upon different aspects of the dispute. The bankrupt and his wife, who had been turned out by force of a Chancery commission in support of Allen, died of the plague in London during July, 1610, leaving seven children, one of whom was "sucking at nurse." The lord chancellor thus received an extra responsibility by virtue of the special care for children reposed in him. "The pitiful cries of the father and mother (dying as is aforesaid) and of the poor orphans do call to God for relief and moved the heart of the lord chancellor." The case was reopened on behalf of the children, and Francis Moore, who had been on the Commons committee in 1604, was assigned as their counsel. John Tyndall, the Chancery master who was repeatedly involved in this matter, eventually produced a report which was the basis of a new Chancery decree. Allen and his friend were to receive their costs, but the proportional agreement reached by the bankruptcy commissioners was incorporated in the decree. Allen could keep the lands and pay over the additional value, or part with the lands and share with other creditors and the children in the profits. He refused to make the required election, and so late in 1613 another decree was issued. This, while still considerate towards Allen and his associate, was more favorable towards the children and other creditors. Allen was still to receive his costs, and debts due to him were to be paid at a rate decided by Tyndall, which some called generous. However, the lands were to be reconveyed to the benefit of all the creditors according to the composition, and it was calculated that this would leave £600 for the children. The Chancery bench and the bankruptcy commissioners were now in line with their priorities.

Allen was committed when he refused to perform the above decree. He subsequently produced two "judgments" in the Common Pleas for the entire debt owing to him which had been entered *after* the bankruptcy commission had been sued out and which had not, of course, been executed. It would be argued that he had not dwelt upon these in the course of the Chancery proceedings, or even mentioned them in his original bill and subsequent pleadings. He went on to claim that his freehold was being called in question by Chancery, and that this was contrary to Magna

[63] P.R.O., C.24/292, no. 12, Bird v. Carrell.

[64] There is a wealth of manuscript sources, including El. 5935–5936; Additional 11,596, f. 118 *et seq.*; Harleian 4265, p. 78 *et seq.* I have not had the time to trace through the most obvious and major source, the Chancery records. For this and related cases, see: J. P. Dawson, "Coke and Ellesmere Disinterred: The Attack on the Chancery in 1616," *Illinois Law Review* **36** (1941): pp. 127–152; J. H. Baker, "The Common Lawyers and the Chancery: 1616," *The Irish Jurist* **4** (1969): pp. 368–392; L. A. Knafla, *Law and Politics in Jacobean England* (Cambridge, 1977), pp. 155–181. This case, as perhaps the most important in the history of English bankruptcy, received more attention than any other from Goodinge, pp. 156–163.

Carta. Yet he had been one of those responsible for suing out the bankruptcy commission, and he had initiated proceedings in Chancery. Abusing the procedures of both commission and court, he was interpreted as trying to defraud his fellow creditors and the bankrupt's children in a fashion which was described as barbarous, covetous, and unconscionable.

The central point was that once bankruptcy had been declared, whatever the complications, Allen could not seek execution on judgments. The latter were suspended until distribution of the available assets had been completed. Thereafter they could be used against anything left over, but this avenue, particularly with respect to the children, was blocked by Chancery.

Allen's Case is renowned. It helped to lure an enthusiastic Coke into trouble, and it played a part in the jurisdictional disputes of 1615 and 1616. The questions raised by this case were similar to those found in others, notably with respect to arguments over Chancery activity after judgment at law. There were other cases and other men. Most of the issues then contested so fiercely, and Allen's subsequent activities, lie outside the scope of this study, as do many events in which Bacon, Coke, and Ellesmere were involved. The case is singular because it contained a number of specific elements which were clear by 1613. Up to a point, Chancery could claim priority of suit on the basis of Allen's own bill of complaint, but this was of minor import. Most crucial was the degree to which the lord chancellor was acting on the basis of responsibilities which were not intrinsic to the court of Chancery. These included his duty to protect the interests of orphaned infants. Hence Tyndall in his deliberations was required to keep an eye on anything which could be done for their relief. Even more significant, however much the situation may have been confused by commissioners and their composition, was the bankruptcy matter. The activities of bankruptcy commissioners might be challenged and found wanting at law, but they were vested firmly in statute. Hence it had already been recognized that a debt assigned by such a commission became "a debt transferred by Parliament." [65] Allen was trying to upset the dispositions of bankruptcy commissioners. When he tried to secure execution on judgments made after the action which constituted bankruptcy, he was trying to evade the intention of statute. Eventually the lord chancellor, as the statutory authority who had granted the commission, acted to preserve the intent of bankruptcy legislation.

It has been seen that in circumstances of both bankruptcy and debt there was considerable anxiety lest one or more creditors, possibly through arrangements with the debtor, might secure repayment at the expense of other creditors. It seems probable that Allen had been preparing the ground in such a direction. Late in Elizabeth's reign, William Lambarde had suggested that Chancery should become more involved in stopping this kind of thing. He also thought that existing legal procedures and conventions were inadequate. In a case involving the goods and debts of an intestate, one party was owed £50 but Lambarde wondered if the court really intended that this should be paid if other creditors received nothing in consequence. His own view was that there ought to be a system for proportional satisfaction, "being the fittest means (in so weak an estate of the deceased) to make conscionable satisfaction of such as he died indebted." [66] In other words, the problem could arise even without collusion. It was particularly acute when, as in the above case, the debtor had died and his remaining resources were insufficient. In circumstances far less extreme than these, many people advocated composition either in terms of further time or of reducing and perhaps sharing the total sum. Yet to do this, and follow Lambarde's suggestion that Chancery should arrange proportional or considerate settlements, would only be possible if dissenting creditors were restrained from exacting their legitimate rights.

One of the difficulties implicit in this situation was that recorded obligations—recognizances, statutes staple, statutes merchant—had the same quality as judgments handed down in open court. Indeed they were judgments which the "debtor" acknowledged in advance. They were obligations of record, conditional or future judgments, and hence in later language statutes merchant were often known as "pocket judgments." Naturally there were many variants, notably with respect to the giving or confessing of acknowledgment and subsequent procedure ranging from execution to action of debt upon the obligation. Even so, there was a distinction of both common sense and technicality between such forms and final judgments handed down in open court. Coke described the practical difference:

> Although both are records, yet the judgment in the King's court upon judicial and ordinary proceeding is more notorious and conspicuous, and of more high and eminent degree than a statute or recognizance taken in private, and by consent of the parties, and therefore preferred in judgment of law before a recognizance or statute. . . .[67]

Recorded and enrolled bonds of this nature were the most important contract mechanisms of the Tudor and early Stuart period. Sometimes, they repre-

[65] Cro. Jac., 105, The Case of Bradshaw (1605).

[66] See above, p. 30. P.R.O., C.38/4, Gybson v. Lownde (1600).

[67] 4 Co. Rep., 60*a*. See generally W. J. Jones, "An Introduction to Petty Bag Proceedings in the Reign of Elizabeth I," *California Law Review* 51 (1963): pp. 882–905.

sented real debts or the sureties for debts, but they also covered a wide range of undertakings from business matters to hunting expeditions. Attempts to block execution provided much business to English bill courts, whether established at Westminster or in the provinces and palatines.[68]

The irony in the situation is that there are indications that Lord Chancellor Ellesmere had been laying down ground rules, in effect restrictions, to govern the kind of relief allowed by Chancery. Long before 1615, he had complained about the number of persons in execution upon judgment for debt or damages who were allowed freedom from prison on the surety of a relative, or temporarily released from custody by *habeas corpus*. This, he stated, encouraged them to take no care to meet their debts.[69] As far as his own court was concerned, he could be more positive. In October, 1614, it was ordered that injunctions were not to issue to stay proceedings after judgment, verdict, and issue unless Chancery had priority of suit and proceedings there had been effectively pursued. Bills of complaint to stay payment of debts due on recorded bonds (or, for that matter, conditions broken on leases and mortgages) were not to be considered if there was evidence of willful default or gross negligence.[70] A number of litigants, including Allen —that he was fraudulent should not cloud the issue— helped to produce a crisis.

The confrontation on grounds of jurisdiction which exploded in 1615 and 1616, and to which the names of Coke and Ellesmere are attached, was at least partly occasioned by political circumstances. Genuine legal matters were raised, but it was not simply a conflict between these two judges. Moreover, issues presented were not always those for which either had prepared himself. They may even have thought alike on some of the points which attracted attention. However, the question of jurisdiction had been raised, and it could not be avoided. One result was an affirmation of Chancery jurisdiction, drafted by Bacon and inspired by Ellesmere: that plaintiffs had a right "to be relieved according to equity and conscience after judgments in the courts of common law in cases where the judges of the common law could not relieve them." [71]

After the rumpus of 1616, the nature of Chancery powers was ostensibly unchanged. Yet its ability to intervene after judgment at law had been upheld and defined.[72] On this basis, Francis Bacon tried to build a systematic policy for the relief of debtors.

Bankruptcy was a means whereby the creditors shared available assets. During the life of the commission the bankrupt could, if allowed, earn money toward payment of his remaining debts. The notion of composition was always present and possible but was not mentioned by the statutes, and there was no discharge. This was deplored by an Elizabethan commentator: "For as the execution of the statute taketh from the bankrupt all that he hath to the utter overthrow of him and his family and the creditors commonly not half paid, so good compositions bringeth in time full payment to the creditors and preservation to the poor men." It has already been seen that compositions on a ratable basis were encouraged by such late Elizabethan lawyers as Lambarde, and there are occasional instances in which creditors seem to have been required to compound. The Privy Council might forward such an arrangement. The real possibility, however, was that a regular relationship might be established between composition, bankruptcy commissions, and the court of Chancery. In a disordered fashion, these elements became conjoined in *Allen's Case*, but the notion was older. In the mid-1590's, one debtor agreed with creditors on a composition for repayment at the rate of two-thirds in the pound, but dissenting creditors had him arrested and forced him to enter a statute for payment of the full debts owing to them. The other creditors, therefore, took out a bankruptcy commission which seized the assets; their rivals proceeded with execution and took out an extent upon the statute. A bill was exhibited in Chancery and an injunction issued to stop the execution.[73]

There was nothing new about conformity and composition. Various compositions and methods of conformity were commonly arranged in the city of London, usually by license but sometimes in collaboration with commissioners of bankruptcy. More generally the procedure of bill of conformity, it was said, had originally developed in the court of Requests before this avenue was blocked by prohibitions. It was then adopted in Chancery by Ellesmere who was "very wary in granting" such petitions, doing so only "in case of extremity." However, a significant aspect of Bacon's control of the Chancery bench in the brief period, 1617–1621, was the way in which he tried to associate the impulse towards composition with conformity among creditors, and also tried to make this burgeoning system apply to situations of bankruptcy. The resulting situation was deemed deplorable by many. "Of late much lenity has been used to all

[68] There were other means, such as *audita querela*, which might be of help in combating or delaying a creditor who sued out execution upon a recorded obligation, but most of these methods had little relevance to the particular circumstances being considered here.

[69] El. 2623. Knafla, p. 276.

[70] Sanders 1, i: pp. 86–87.

[71] *Ibid.* 1, i: p. 90.

[72] Decades later, Nottingham referred to the "exploded opinion" that to sue in Chancery after judgment was a *praemunire*. *Nottingham's Cases* 2: p. 870.

[73] P.R.O., S.P.12/146, no. 125. I. Treiman, "Majority Control in Compositions: Its Historical Origins and Development," *Virginia Law Review* 24 (1938): p. 519.

debtors, so that many [creditors], after four or five years suit and charges in this court, were glad to go away with their principal without costs or damages." [74]

Any attempt to arrange a composition, even if it was just with the standard intention of providing further time, meant that influence had to be used against creditors who wished to secure an immediate and full recovery of what was owing. The situation was eased when a commission had been sued out under the bankruptcy statutes. This was because the creditors' ability had been suspended by legislation. Even so, there was always the possibility of difficulty occasioned by creditors who chose not to join or who flouted agreements. Allen illustrates the point: he had asked for and joined with the commission, but he had not found its arrangements to his liking. If his position had been maintained, the system of bankruptcy proceedings would have been undermined.

In 1620, one case concerned a debtor and his creditors who had agreed on payment through installments spread over a period of years. However, a single creditor persuaded the debtor to enter a statute merchant as additional security which would give him a legal advantage if the debtor defaulted. Consequently, the other creditors sued out a bankruptcy commission. In any case, the first installment was not paid on time and the statute merchant was put into execution. The greater part of the estate was extended. Turning to Chancery, the other creditors obtained an order that the extent was to be stayed, the statute merchant was to be surrendered, and the bankruptcy commission was to proceed without hindrance.[75] It is not entirely clear whether the recent agreement was abrogated. This may have been so because the debtor should not have made a commitment to one man which threatened the interests of other creditors. However, it is possible that the bankruptcy commission was expected to confirm the agreement. It was, after all, a year which witnessed the climax of Bacon's policy of conformity.

Building on the long-established sense that some situations were unfair, Bacon tried to create a coherent system. Success would have meant the establishment of a new segment of procedure and jurisdiction; indeed it was a complaint of critics in 1621 that this had already happened. The idea was that majority groups of creditors, representing at least two-thirds of the sum due, would petition in Chancery to compel the other creditors into joining a ratable composition or provision for further time. These bills of conformity might have been impossible had not Chancery's powers after judgment at law been so unequivocally explained in 1616.

The case of *Tiffin v. Hart*, 1618–1619, concerned an insolvent who died leaving a debt of over £9,800, most of which was secured by bonds. His sons offered to surrender both his and their estates, valued at £5,500, if the creditors would accept a proportionate settlement in full discharge. Few were willing, but after a petition to the king, who set up a committee, the creditors were divided on this offer: fifty-five accepted, but twenty-five (who were owed less than twenty-five per cent of the total) refused and commenced action at law. The sons and the majority group of creditors countered with a bill in Chancery and secured an injunction for stay of the proceedings at law. After a second petition to the king, which was referred to the lord chancellor, it was subsequently held that the dissenting creditors were to be bound by the agreement of the majority. The only exception was that those who had advanced money held in trust for infants, or free of interest, were to be repaid in full by specified installments.[76]

Creditors who refused composition might be "unreasonable," [77] but often some had lent money on terms more generous and less profitable to themselves than was the case with those who were willing to accept a composition. Such people were irritated by Bacon's policy of enforcing conformity and enraged by his apparent readiness to imprison dissenters.

One debtor had been allowed further time by the majority of his creditors, but their bill of conformity was rejected when they failed to rebut a defense motion for dismissal. Probably this was a procedural error. In consequence, the king was petitioned. He referred the matter to the bishop of London and three others who were described as "a commission in the nature of a commission of bankruptcy." They concluded that none of the creditors could receive satisfaction unless further time was given. The matter came back into Chancery where it was decided that the debtor was to be given four years in which to

[74] Tothill, 47, Mildmay v. Wentworth (1613). *APC* 1590, p. 98. *Common Debates 1621* **5**: p. 39; **6**: pp. 63–64. T. Powel, *The Mysterie of Lending and Borrowing* (London, 1623), pp. 11, 18, 51. Turner, *Equity of Redemption*, p. 31.

[75] J. Ritchie, *Reports of Cases Decided by Francis Bacon, 1617–21* (London, 1932) pp. 165–166, Overman v. Wright (1620). See the Elizabethan case above, at n. 73.

[76] *Ibid.*, pp. 161–164.

[77] *Ibid.*, p. 165, Ryder v. Turner (1617). One who benefited was Sir Henry Finch, serjeant-at-law, who had served as a referee in *Tiffin v. Hart.* He became insolvent, but although his only means of repayment was through his profession, the creditors had brought actions on the bonds against him and his sons. *Ibid.*, pp. 166–167, Finch v. Hicks (1620). In 1621, this case was instanced by Coke and Cranfield as an appalling example. Prestwich, pp. 299–300. Some years later his son, John Finch, the future chief justice and lord keeper, who had agreed to pay what was owing, received a protection for one year from arrest for debt. P.R.O., S.P.39/14, no. 66.

meet his obligations, and in the meantime actions at law, including those against his sureties, were stayed.[78]

Whatever its "nature," the commission appointed in the above case cannot be regarded as a commission of bankruptcy. The affair, however, seems to fit in with a procedural device which was being developed. Most plaintiffs maintained their suits in Chancery, but the court did not really want to imprison defendants who resisted composition. A formula might be constructed in those instances where the debtor could be declared a bankrupt. The majority creditors, in association with the debtor, would submit a bill of conformity in Chancery, subsequently petitioning the lord chancellor for a bankruptcy commission. This would be granted, but the petitioners would be asked to secure a binding and final composition. Since the majority creditors were already agreed, this would not cause difficulty. Minority creditors, those who opposed composition, could either come to heel and join or remain aloof and risk recovering nothing. The settlement arranged by the bankruptcy commission, which by itself had no authority to make a final composition, would be confirmed by the Chancery, which had prior jurisdiction because of the bill of conformity. Those clauses of the bankruptcy statutes which made it possible for creditors to take their own legal initiatives, once the commission had done its work, would thus be negated.[79]

A clever procedure had been developed to support the notion that a bankruptcy commission, where feasible, should try to secure a composition. This was just a little segment of the policy of conformity sustained by Bacon from 1617. He himself had known what it was like to live under almost unbearable stress as a debtor. Furthermore, his brief period as lord keeper and then as lord chancellor, 1617–1621,[80] coincided with a shattering depression. Business failures were widespread, landed men were suffering, workers were unemployed, and creditors were rarely in a worse position to insist upon complete and individual satisfaction. In trying to produce a procedure to meet situations which many had previously considered absurd, Bacon had the advantage that Chancery's position had recently been clarified. But his approach was not liked. The former warden of the Fleet claimed that Chancery had become more lavish in granting writs of *habeas corpus* to aid debtors. On the other hand, he opined that although hardly any creditors were actually restrained because of bills of conformity, the very possibility aroused anger and apprehension: "Creditors were in dread of those bills and were against those bills for fear they might be imprisoned and checked in their prosecution of debtors. . . ."[81] Hostility was expressed by people who had immediate reason to feel that they had been wronged, and by those who believed that all bills of conformity gave unjustifiable encouragement to willful debtors. In these years of slump, some claimed that bills of conformity invited foreigners to withdraw their capital and interests from England.[82] It was easy to portray the predicament of minority creditors as a denial of justice. They could lose money or even end up in prison merely for trying to obtain their due on the basis of contracts, judgments, and obligations which had been entered into freely.

It is the above contradiction which makes arguments of 1620–1621 more poignant than those of 1615–1616. On the previous occasion, the debate had been largely fortuitous. Now it was a genuine clash, enhanced but not created by the slump, between a reasoned expectation of legal forms and a conscious attempt to limit the effect of these forms. In the summer of 1620, James I was petitioned by Londoners to do something about bills of conformity.[83] In October, Bacon issued orders which refined and limited the conditions under which they might be considered: "that no compulsory order be granted to enforce creditors to conform themselves and agree unto any rate or composition at the suit or petition of the debtor or insolvent himself but only at the suit of the creditors in imitation and according to the equity of the statute of bankrupts." Petitioning creditors now had to represent three-quarters of the sum due. There were other limitations, and in any case Chancery would only proceed with great caution. Bacon, however, was still clinging to his fundamental principle: it was possible to link the social justification for composition in matters of debt with the restricted but explicit notions of bankruptcy.[84]

This was only one of the issues which Bacon had to face in 1621. Had this been all, he might have been able to ride out the storm and even justify bills of conformity on grounds of social need. Only it was not all. Bacon was implicated in the onslaught upon the referees, the Chancery was under general attack because of its complexity and cost, and Buckingham was not prepared to risk himself to save the lord chancellor. Bacon was charged with taking gratuities. Chancery was accused of damaging commerce. A member of Parliament voiced the idea that although a predecessor had helped to create the problem, the consequences "will proceed from Chancellor to Chancery."[85] Bacon was under fire from too many directions. On 31 March, a royal proclamation provided

[78] Ritchie, pp. 191–192, Brooke v. Goode (1619).

[79] *Ibid.*, p. 193, Bourne v. Ironmonger (1619).

[80] Bacon received the higher title on 4 January, 1618.

[81] A. Harris. *The Œconomy of the Fleete*, ed. A. Jessup, Camden Soc., new ser. 25 (1879), pp. 107–109.

[82] *Commons Debates 1621* 7: p. 581.

[83] *Ibid.* 4: p. 67.

[84] Sanders 1, i: pp. 129–131.

[85] *CJ* 1: p. 573.

that bills of conformity were to be dismissed unless all the creditors had consented, and new bills were not to be received. On 18 April, this was implemented by a Chancery order. The possibility of using Chancery or any other court (others were covered by the proclamation) to arrange a composition was not totally erased. Henceforth, however, petitioning creditors would have to represent three-quarters of the sum owing, acceptance would have to be achieved without compulsion, and the debtor was not to be a petitioner.[86]

In 1624, the critics completed their victory. Under the new bankruptcy statue, a person who sought a composition for further time was liable to become a bankrupt, assuming that his trade or means of livelihood made this possible, unless he made his approach in good time and with the utmost propriety. Otherwise a debtor could, by the very attempt at negotiation with creditors, be construed as having committed an act of bankruptcy. In these circumstances, a minority of creditors might petition for a commission of bankruptcy, and as yet no one had said that the lord chancellor could refuse such a request. Thus subsequently it is possible to find victims, such as an unfortunate feltmaker, once employing dozens but now fallen on bad times, who was imprisoned for debt. Fifteen of his creditors agreed to give him respite for four years, but the remaining two refused and obtained a bankruptcy commission.[87]

NOTTINGHAM

In the 1630's, Lord Keeper Coventrye and the Privy Council tried to probe the situation, but they could not produce any concrete reappraisals. Interpretation of the statutory system belonged increasingly to the judges, and this was so whether under monarchy or republic. It was apparent that some tricky questions had been posed, but these did not receive positive answers. It cannot be said that they were even accorded serious analysis.

First and foremost, there was the old conundrum of the lord chancellor's authority. Under the Henrician statute, it is clear that jurisdiction in all ways was directly in the hands of those who had power to act, and the lord chancellor was always the most prominent of these and probably the effective agent in practice. If he chose to appoint commissioners to do the job, this was out of necessity and convenience. The Elizabethan statute, however, specifically mentioned the appointment of commissioners. During the hundred years after 1571, the lord chancellor seems on occasion to have made or unmade commissions and tried to ensure that these did not abuse their position. On the other hand, it does not appear that he reviewed their decisions.[88] No one was absolutely sure if the chancellor could refuse a request for a commission, and certainly there was no clear idea as to the extent of his authority once a commission had issued. But if the authority of the chancellor was in any way vague, it followed that the authority of the commissioners was equally amorphous. The situation was abominably obscure, and Holdsworth had natural difficulties in trying to explain the structure of authority created by the 1571 act. This "gave to the chancellor power to appoint, by commission under the Great Seal, certain persons to exercise the powers of the chancellor over the person and property of the bankrupt. The act gave no jurisdiction in bankruptcy to the court of Chancery. It gave the chancellor no control over the commissioners." The chancellor might seem to be no more than the statutory, administrative means through which a satisfactory commission could be appointed. Could it then be said that the commissioners were exercising his power? This, of course, was the kind of point which Coke tried to explain to James I when it was a matter of debating judicial independence, but it is unlikely that such sophistication was applied to the comparatively miniscule circumstance of bankruptcy commissioners.[89]

In practice, most chancellors were uncertain about their authority and were cautious in their actions, but hardly anyone thought that a commission of bankruptcy had a judicial status distinct from the power of the chancellor. In the reign of Charles II, Nottingham cut through the tangle by deciding that the grant of a commission of bankruptcy was analogous to the grant of a commission of sewers. He then proceeded to demolish this conclusion as undesirable.[90]

---

[86] Sanders 1, i: pp. 132–134. Lansdowne 569, f. 26. Despite these restrictions, it was claimed that debtors still found means to restrain their creditors. *Commons Debates 1621* **7**: pp. 581–582.

[87] Treiman, "Majority Control," p. 521.

[88] *Nottingham's Cases* **1**: p. cxv. In a case already noted, the lord chancellor suspended the proceedings of a commission by ordering issue of a *supersedeas*. A *procedendo*, permitting continuation, was later awarded. Monro, p. 286.

[89] Holdsworth **1**: p. 470. Holdsworth presumed that in the seventeenth century commissioners who were in legal difficulty "applied" to the common law courts. The degree to which this was true is uncertain, but in any case action by the chancellor or proceedings in Chancery were not excluded. Most of the legal difficulties experienced resulted in the commissioners appearing as defendants and pleading the authority of their commission in actions with respect to which the chancellor could be of little help.

[90] *Nottingham's 'Manual'*, p. 161. The impact of Nottingham's work can be seen in Blackstone's conclusion (**3**: p. 427) that the lord chancellor had a summary jurisdiction "in many matters consequential or previous to the commissions. . . ." Holdsworth (**1**: p. 471), describing the eighteenth-century situation, went a little too far: "Original jurisdiction was exercised by commissioners. Their appointment was in the absolute control of the lord chancellor; but when appointed he had no control over them." According to

Nottingham began by acknowledging that there was complete uncertainty as to whether the lord chancellor had discretion to grant or refuse a commission. He accepted that the power to grant, based upon the 1571 statute, might be interpreted as implying that there must be a right of denial. He was also aware that several *caveats*, against granting commissions until the arguments of the parties had been heard, were entered during Coventrye's lord keepership. However, his conclusion, aided by a decision of 1647–1648, was that the application represented a petition of right. This could not be refused and the commissions were granted *de jure*. In addition, and despite varying precedents, he concluded that the lord chancellor could not grant a limited or qualified commission.[91]

Nottingham would have made a good historian. On the evidence of the past, he was capable of reaching an interpretation which was repugnant to him. He then commented unfavorably on the situation:

> This makes the commissioners of bankruptcy very untractable and hard to be regulated, because they think they have authority by act of Parliament and though they execute it never so extravagantly, yet they need fear no control but that of an action against them at law.

He suggested that the lord chancellor should have the power to "supersede" a commission "if they proceed indiscreetly." Though what had been done could not be undone, a new commission of "wiser men" could handle the remaining business.[92]

Nottingham was most concerned with those situations when the indiscretion and ill-doings of the commissioners had become apparent. Even so, action should only be taken after due consideration and examination. If the bankrupt and all the creditors were satisfied that the commissioners were behaving improperly, a petition for a *supersedeas* should be allowed. If the petition was not unanimous, however, extreme care was needed for fear of collusion. In this circumstance, suggested Nottingham, the commissioners should be asked how far they had proceeded. Only if the four-month period, before which distribution could not begin, was not completed, or nearly so, should a *supersedeas* issue.[93]

Nottingham's analysis and the procedure proposed opened the way for a new jurisdiction. He was cautious, and he was reluctant to grant appeals from statutory jurisdictions. He seems to have believed that the speed of remedy offered usually outweighed most grievances. He did hear a complaint that the commissioners had not allowed proof of a debt, but he was doubtful, since the commissioners were liable to an action at law. The precedent, he feared, might result in the execution of all bankruptcy commissions being inspected.[94] There can be little doubt that Nottingham intended supervision to be exercised with restraint, but the culmination of his work was the development in Chancery of an appellate bankruptcy jurisdiction.

AFTER NOTTINGHAM

From the end of the seventeenth century, the lord chancellor's interest in the affairs of bankrupts and bankruptcy commissions was gradually extended. There was also a renewal of statutory activity, and legislation in the reign of Anne really indicates the start of a new chapter. Most notable was a statute late in her reign which voided existing descriptions of a bankrupt.[95] One novelty was the bankrupt's certificate of discharge, which could be allowed by the lord chancellor or any two judges to whom he referred the matter.[96] By another statute, the commissioners were required to assign the bankrupt's effects to persons picked by the creditors. These assignees, construed in law as trustees, were subject to the chancellor's equitable jurisdiction, and proceedings by English bill could be commenced against them in the normal fashion.[97] In 1732, they were declared to be officials of the Great Seal. Then and subsequently, their duties were clarified: collection of the bankrupt's effects, payment of dividends, and presentation to the commissioners of proper accounts for receipts and expenditures. Under certain circumstances the chancellor, if petitioned by creditors, could dismiss the assignees or suspend the commission.[98]

The chancellor's control over bankruptcy proceedings had been recognized by statute. In practice, he would continue to work through his court, and Chancery's involvement with bankruptcy matters apparently increased radically from the 1730's. It has been suggested that this was encouraged, at least in part, by an awareness of the large fees which thereby accrued

---

Montagu, the issue of commissions and all questions arising were the original jurisdiction of the lord chancellor. However, execution of commissions was given to commissioners who were assistant judges provided by Parliament for the lord chancellor. Whether the lord chancellor had a direct jurisdiction was uncertain, but Montagu thought that this was probably so since he could make an order on a petition just as he could make a decree in Chancery. B. Montagu, *Inquiries*.

[91] *Nottingham's 'Manual'*, pp. 161–162. The word "may" was construed as "must": the lord chancellor "must" grant a commission. 1 Eq. Ca. Abr., 52.

[92] *Nottingham's 'Manual'*, p. 162.

[93] *Ibid.*, p. 164.

[94] *Nottingham's Cases* **1**: pp. cxiii–cxvi, 313.

[95] 10 Anne c. 25.

[96] 4 and 5 Anne c. 4. Holdsworth (**1**: p. 470), on the authority of C. P. Cooper, concluded that the chancellor usually referred this matter to the judges, until Hardwicke's time (1737–1757).

[97] 6 Anne c. 22.

[98] Holdsworth **1**: p. 470. 5 George II c. 30.

to the chancellor.[99] In 1831, as part of a general move towards reorganization of the court of Chancery, some attempt was made to improve the situation. Jurisdiction in bankruptcy was transferred from the lord chancellor to a chief judge in bankruptcy, who was to be assisted by three judges and six commissioners. The line of appeal was to a court of review and then to the lord chancellor,[100] but in 1847 this court of review was abolished and its jurisdiction given to a vice-chancellor.[101]

The flaw in Nottingham's inheritance should have been apparent to later chancellors and to legislators, at least from the reign of Anne. The chancellor's ability to exercise his powers and initiative weakened under the monolithic slowness of eighteenth and early nineteenth-century Chancery proceedings. Bankruptcy questions were just one more burden, and Montagu noted that in the early nineteenth century Chancery business was constantly interrupted by such matters.[102] It would, however, be false to pinpoint a single area of jurisdicion. The problems of Chancery were far greater than that. This was a tribunal which was clearly overworked and which had never struggled free from the complex machinery of pleading and proof bestowed upon it by Elizabethan chancellors. That this endowment was vital to its position is a standard contradiction of modern administrative development. In these conditions, adequate control over the bankruptcy commissioners, who exercised original jurisdiction, was not in fact possible. This partly explains why bankruptcy commissioners acquired a scandalous reputation because of their charges, their apparent ability to become principal beneficiaries from the estates of bankrupts, and their capacity to evade statutes aimed at limiting reprehensible habits.[103] Equally disturbing was the widespread evasion of bankruptcy proceedings by debtors.[104] Lists of commissioners of bankruptcy existed in London, and though there were not at first similar lists for the rest of the country, the situation seems to have been equally appalling. Eradication of this state of affairs became a major concern of nineteenth-century legal reformers. In 1869, the London court of bankruptcy was established, and the situation was again transformed by the Judicature Act of 1873. The county commissioners were replaced by local bankruptcy courts, and these were eventually superseded by the county courts.[105]

Debtors in seventeenth-century Massachusetts, as in England, had no procedure approaching the modern discharge of bankruptcy, and they were probably even more helpless than those in the mother country with respect to their ability to secure a composition.[106] After the revolution, the bankruptcy laws of the United States continued to be an offspring of Tudor and Stuart ideas. However, article I, section 8, of the constitution, ratified in June, 1788, contained a commitment to establish uniform laws with respect to bankruptcies. An act of 1800, repealed after three years, applied only to traders, but legislation of 1841, also repealed shortly, and the important act of 1867 applied to persons other than traders and merchants.[107] By this time, the United Kingdom Parliament had also moved in the same direction.

Early eighteenth-century legislation in England reveals some changes in attitudes. The very idea of a discharge, although itself a source of abuse, must have done something to solve the old problem of further liability on which so many attempts at composition had foundered. Statute even permitted an allowance for maintenance to be made to a bankrupt who surrendered promptly.[108] There may well have been some sympathy, but if so, it was checked by the somewhat severe provisions of the 1732 statute, passed during a period when considerable additions were being made to the list of capital offenses.[109] Thereafter, a string of statutes tackled a variety of problems: wages, estates tail, arrears of rent, and so on.[110] In 1847, a court for the relief of insolvent debtors was set up. This was designed to assist insolvents who were not merchants or traders

[99] Holdsworth 1: p. 471. For a comment on Mansfield and the activities of the King's Bench in hearing references from the chancellors or actions brought by receivers, see Harding, p. 317.

[100] 1 and 2 William IV c. 56.

[101] Holdsworth 1: p. 443. 10 and 11 Victoria c. 102, *2. The statute of 6 George IV c. 16 had repealed existing bankruptcy legislation and consolidated the bankruptcy laws.

[102] Montagu, *Inquiries*.

[103] The 1705 statute inhibited allowance for "eating and drinking" by the commissioners and others at meetings of creditors. 4 and 5 Anne c. 4, *21.

[104] J. H. T. Hughes, *Fluctuations in Trade, Industry and Finance: A Study of British Economic Development, 1850–1860* (Oxford, 1960), p. 33.

[105] Holdsworth 1: pp. 444, 471–473.

[106] However, other rules concerning debtors "were far in advance of contemporary English practice." G. L. Haskins, *Law and Authority in Early Massachusetts* (New York, 1960), pp. 215–220, 286.

[107] Teevan and Smith, p. 953. For a brief account of events, see C. Warren, *Bankruptcy in United States History* (Cambridge, Mass., 1935). In the last quarter of the nineteenth century, some felt that there was a disturbing swing in favor of creditors. The case for voluntary bankruptcy was argued in the House of Representatives by a lawyer who felt that this trend should be restrained. F. G. Newlands, *Bankruptcy, its Cause and Remedy* (Washington, 1896).

[108] 4 and 5 Anne c. 4, *8.

[109] See Jenks, pp. 384–388. The establishment of the death penalty for non-surrender and concealment occasioned few prosecutions and, in a period of almost ninety years, only about four executions. The overall trend towards severity must not be exaggerated. A statute of 1774, describing many bankrupts and debtors as well-meaning but unfortunate, asserted that such "have always been deemed the proper objects of public compassion." 14 George III c. 77.

[110] Jenks, pp. 384–385.

and who could not be made bankrupt. The idea was that they could escape imprisonment for debt by surrendering their property.[111] The device indicates the degree to which bankruptcy had gradually come to be seen as having distinct advantages for the debtor. The surprising thing is that, once the discharge had been introduced, it should have taken so long for bankruptcy principles to be extended beyond those who lived through buying and selling, and even after 1847 variations were still played on the ancient theme of occupational distinction. The comprehensive statute of 1849, while introducing several new rules, made little breach in the durability of this particular legacy.[112] Only in 1861 was the distinction between traders and non-traders abolished.[113] Married women were still excluded, and a statute of 1869 confined its "voluntary settlement" clause to traders.[114]

By the mid-nineteenth century the game laws, another species of regulation, had undergone revision. They have been described as "a privilege conferred by a ruling class on itself merely as a perquisite of ruling"; change occurred when "the rule of the landed of which those laws were the symbol" weakened.[115] Whereas the game laws had excluded most classes of men from hunting, the bankruptcy laws had confined one category within a particular set of rules affecting the payment of debts. There were, of course, major differences between the two positions. But if it can be argued that the game laws, whatever their economic value, symbolized a social privilege, the bankruptcy laws came to represent certain privileges, notably the discharge, which could be of advantage to other classes of men.

English bankruptcy had its inception in four Tudor and early Stuart statutes. The law then created was penal in character, and there is no need to quarrel with contemporaries who conceived that the statutes were made against certain categories of debtor. The idea of helping bankrupts was not present. It must be asked how far these attitudes were a product of the contemporary social structure and its assumptions.

V. GENTLEMEN, LAWYERS, MERCHANTS, AND TRADESMEN

A clear expansion of England's economy only occurred in the second half of the seventeenth century. Earlier, despite an initial and spurious prosperity for the first decade of James's reign, there was often little confidence and much gloom. The 1624 bankruptcy statute was framed in this atmosphere, and yet it would have to do service in the more halcyon days of the Restoration. Furthermore, the commissioners were hampered by restraints and inadequacies, bearable and even understandable prior to the 1650's, which demanded revision.

The central conundrum, although founded on unavoidable statute law, can only be described in social terms: everything had come to depend upon the assumption that it was feasible to make a differential analysis of men according to their occupations, sources of income, and modes of life. The statutes themselves provided labels, but they did little in the way of providing definitions. In consequence, the commissioners sometimes occupied a no-man's-land between the label and the task of determining what it meant. However, the situation can be stated crudely: if a person could be construed as living by buying and selling, and if he committed an act which had been specified by the bankruptcy statutes, then his prospects were governed by procedures which did not apply to others. A peculiar department had been created within the varied laws and rules of debt. It was a legal distinction, but it was also a social one.

Any bankrupt is and was a person unable to back his formerly assumed credit with cash. Accountancy books and manuals have been cited as evidence for the development of credit organization in late Tudor England, but it would be difficult to assert that techniques of banking and credit were seen by contemporaries as adequate.[1] On the other hand, merchants were practical: they only relied upon such credit facilities as were available. Cash was still the favored basis for commercial transactions. Professor Supple has stressed the mobility of mercantile assets and capital in the early Stuart period, and he has illustrated the degree to which hard money was used. This was particularly so in the market for white cloth: merchants generally had to conclude immediate transactions for the purchase of cloth coming up to London.[2] Nonetheless, there were serious limitations. The general rate of interest and profit was probably too low with respect to the long-term average rate of return on trading capital.[3] Merchants, whether creditors or debtors, not uncommonly failed to secure loans, translate assets into cash, or take up money by bills of exchange.

[111] 10 and 11 Victoria c. 102, *4.

[112] 12 and 13 Victoria c. 106.

[113] 24 and 25 Victoria c. 134. This statute abolished the court for the relief of insolvent debtors. The companies act of 1862 coalesced the concepts of joint-stock and incorporation. The principle was reached that a company could go into liquidation but could not be made bankrupt. Cooke, pp. 18, 172.

[114] Jenks, p. 386.

[115] J. H. Hexter, *Reappraisals in History* (New York, 1963), p. 17.

[1] R. D. Richards, *The Early History of Banking* (London, 1929), pp. 20–21.

[2] Supple, pp. 10, 40, 173. It has been suggested that small graziers, lacking capital, purchased sheep on credit and paid after the wool had been sold. Large graziers, capable of extending credit to middlemen and manufacturers, might be in a different situation. Bowden, pp. 13–14.

[3] R. Grassby, "The Rate of Profit in Seventeenth-Century England," *EHR* **84** (1969): pp. 732–733.

Whatever the relationship between cash and credit may have been, living on credit was habitual. Failure to meet obligations, no less than evasion of paying debts, was certainly not confined to merchants and traders. It may be that the landed gentleman, whose flow of income could be irregular, was particularly compelled to rely upon his credit. Those who depended upon lands and tenements might distrust existing banking arrangements, such as they were, and choose to store surplus capital as bullion and plate. At the same time, however, they were exploiting the rules of conveyancing and exploring the subtleties of mortgage and redemption. Furthermore, many of those who borrowed had good credit, and the fact of their borrowing should not be construed as financial difficulty.

Although merchants probably made a greater use of cash than has sometimes been appreciated, it may be that contemporary and landed observers, the parliamentary types, overestimated the extent to which this ability prevailed among *all types* of traders, including those who had to trust the credit of their customers. Likewise, the prosperity of the business community seems to have been magnified in the eyes of others, and this without much appreciation either of distinctions of wealth, and thus of opportunities for profit within that community, or of the much vaguer but nonetheless real distinctions of rank between the various styles of trading. The bankruptcy statutes seem to have been based upon the assumption that traders pressed to repay debts should be able to find cash, possibly by selling assets, or be able to provide some suitable alternative. If this was not so, a bankruptcy commission might take over and do the job for them. The implication was that excuses or requests for extra time were likely to be dishonest or futile. There was no provision for the retailer, who bought and sold on credit because he lacked an alternative, or for the merchant who had allowed the bulk of his assets to be tied up, let us suppose safely, in another country. If a ship came home after the appointment of a commission, guidelines had not been provided to govern or encourage termination of the proceedings.

It might be argued that these strictures miss the point. The number of bankruptcy commissions was small in comparison with litigation for recovery of debts or goods. There must be a supposition that in most instances genuine failure had occurred and that bankrupts had lost their credit reputations in the eyes of men of their own kind. It was mostly businessmen who sued out commissions. The trouble was that once an initiative was taken, other creditors had little alternative. Bankruptcy was intimately concerned with the dissolution of a man's credit, a point different from his potential ability or inability to repay all his debts. Delay on the part of hesitant creditors was pointless, and if protracted might result in their exclusion from a share in the fruits of the proceedings. Once the claim of bankruptcy was raised, the only sensible approach was that of "follow the leader."

Whatever advice was given, it was Parliament and not the business community which framed these statutes. Hence bankruptcy law during its first two centuries was welded between two conflicting points of view. The assumptions and attitudes of landed men were sometimes best expressed by lawyers, and mercantile doubt or dissent found expression in the writings of contemporary economic disputants. These different points of view are reflected in the works of Coke and Malynes. At this elevated level, however, little attention was paid to ordinary shopkeepers and traders—the butchers, bakers, and chandlers—although these comprised the overwhelming majority of those who went bankrupt.

Coke's writings are of great importance and even his defects, often as disturbing as they are discernible, cannot detract from the brilliance of the whole or from the particular genius of this tempestuous character. He was proud of never casting "his penny into the water,"[4] and he sometimes had harsh things to say about merchants. This does not mean that he was obtuse, and he probably thought more about economic problems than many other lawyers. The catalog of his library contains fifteen "books of trade," including Wheeler's *Treatise of Commerce*. Other works touched agriculture: these were mostly in Italian, although Tusser was there.[5] Coke, who participated in several cases of commercial interest, was an intelligent and well-read person whose ideas and assumptions may be taken as reasonably representative of the considered mood which lay behind statutes and even government policy. Among privy councillors he alone supported Cockayn's project and with the king completed a trio which promoted that disastrous and probably fraudulent undertaking. The point is not that the bulk of advice was against the project, or that he subsequently turned against it, but that the chief justice was acting as a commercial adviser. Yet his attitude towards the bankruptcy laws, coming as it did from a well-furred elder of the legal profession, may help us to understand why it was that so many merchants wanted to have as little as possible to do with lawyers, their ways, and their logic.

Writing about bankruptcy in the fourth volume of his *Institutes*, composed in the late 1620's, Coke moved dangerously close to that deadly flaw of insularity which could discolor expositions of English law and institutions. "We have fetched as well the name as the wickedness of bankrupts from foreign

[4] Cited, L. Stone, *The Crisis of the Aristocracy, 1558–1641* (Oxford, 1965), p. 377.

[5] *A Catalogue of the Library of Sir Edward Coke*, ed. W. O. Hassall (New Haven, 1950), pp. 80–81, 83, 85.

nations." Granted that this predicament was a matter of statutory creation, he was justified insofar as he conceived that it could not have existed prior to the first bankruptcy statute. Yet he managed to blend this truism into an impression that similar behavior—"bankruptcy" as a socially recognizable circumstance —had also been unknown in England. Apart from a medieval statute which was concerned with Lombards,[6] he took the absence of legislation before 1543 as evidence that Englishmen had behaved with propriety. "In former times as the name of bankrupt, so was the offense itself (as hath been said) a stranger to an Englishman, who of all other nations was freest of bankruptcy."[7]

Coke in this chapter did not consider the possibility that later medieval society had developed procedures inadequate for many peculiarities of debt. It should also be remembered that England, despite certain important branches of commerce, had not been a trading center comparable to Northern Italy, the Low Countries, or Barcelona, where countless mercantile themes and interests could intermingle. He did, however, appreciate that responsibility for subsequent developments could not be placed solely on the shoulders of corrupting continental influences. Those at home had gone astray. Hence Coke, perhaps making an overly literal interpretation of the preamble to the Henrician statute, declared that it had been necessary because English merchants had wallowed in extravagance, "costly building, costly diet, and costly apparel," which had caused them to waste their wealth and neglect their trade.[8]

The charge of extravagance could be laid with equal ease against other ranks in society, notably the highest, but this suspicion about merchants was a common attitude of the time. At the end of the seventeenth century, Sir Richard Cock reflected the same kind of thinking, although he thought that the bankruptcy laws encouraged rather than deterred such appalling behavior. Merchants and traders, he said, were addicted to an expensive and vain style of living. When losses occurred, bankruptcy enabled them "to cheat their creditors, and to give of[f] trading to the ruin of their own and other families and the great damage of the public."[9]

Bankrupts were considered by some as worse than highway robbers and more damaging than foreign enemies.[10] Before the civil wars, John Stone gave a reading on the 1571 statute which associated an increase in the number of merchants with the enhancement of their "cunning and crafty dealings." He had little doubt but that the bankruptcy statutes were justifiably made "against" merchants.[11] Stone acquired a great reputation as a bankruptcy expert which survived into the following century. Thomas Goodinge and E. Green brought his observations up to date and added their own comments, but both applauded and confirmed a principal argument of the reading. They believed that as merchants grew more numerous their behavior deteriorated, and that this decline was initially accelerated because it had been easier for merchants to recover debts from others than it was to recover debts from merchants.[12]

Stone's reading, apart from its brief social comment, is of symbolic importance because the substance of his lecture was concerned with statutory interpretation, judicial precedent, and book law. His concentration upon pre-Elizabethan rules, sometimes utilized in hypothetical cases, illustrates both an apparent weakness of the bankruptcy statutes (he himself was only concerned with that of 1571) and the problems of a legal generation which was seeking to discover precedents from previous ages at a time when the notion of precedent, as understood by men of his own day, was still undergoing birth pangs. This work has hardly the slightest appreciation of commercial issues, the complexities of credit, or fluctuations in the terms of trade. In a duller vein, the approach was to be repeated by Billinghurst's list of statutes and cases concerning bankrupts. This was a practical handbook of legal rules: the atmosphere of the courts is predominant; the odor of the countinghouse is not so much irrelevant as it is ignored.[13]

Among mercantile commentators few paid so much attention to bankruptcy as did Garret de Malynes. He was a practical man of affairs, and something of a rogue, who had known both success and failure. At times he was respected as an expert, but his life had embraced curious paths of litigation. As a debtor, he seems to have been a pretty scurrilous character who plagued his creditors with lawsuits, one who could turn prison into a place of good living and a base for further stratagems. As such he may be considered as one of those who provided ammunition to critics of business behavior. Yet some of his reflections on economic affairs were marked by an interest in the applicability of theoretical propositions. In the early 1620's his advice was sought, and if not sought it was proffered, when problems of trade, the coinage, and the exchanges perplexed government and Parliament. He was particularly concerned with tight credit and

[6] Treiman, "Escaping the Creditor," p. 232. The word *Lombard* was applied to most North Italian merchants, including Venetians, but it was also used generally for moneylenders and pawnbrokers.

[7] Coke, *Fourth Institute*, p. 277.

[8] *Ibid.*

[9] Cited in *Seventeenth-Century Economic Documents*, ed. Joan Thirsk and J. P. Cooper (Oxford, 1972), p. 104.

[10] Lansdowne 99, f. 185.

[11] Stone, *Reading*, p. 3.

[12] Goodinge, preface. E. Green, *The Spirit of the Bankrupt Laws* (London, 1767), preface.

[13] Billinghurst also noted statutes concerned with fraudulent conveyances.

believed that England's difficulties resulted from an undervaluation of her currency, which prompted the export of specie and dramatically affected the foreign exchanges. In order to discuss all this he had to embrace a number of immediate and limited issues, including those posed by bankrupts and debtors. He was perverse, but he remains of interest.[14]

Malynes mused on the extent to which business implied a morality at odds with the ancient and equally traditional concepts of a non-commercial society. General understandings of honesty and dishonesty might be irrelevant to affairs of trade. It was apparent that unthinking behavior on the part of potential debtors and unreasonable pressure from precipitate creditors could lead to trouble. Malynes pointed out the significance of these elements (which Coke ignored), but he argued that the possibility of drifting into a near-bankrupt state arose not so much from the acts of men, however much these might tilt the balance towards disaster, as from the intrinsic nature of the merchant's estate. A single loss at a time when all one's money was laid out could throw an unbearable strain upon the merchant's credit, however sound it might appear to be on paper. Accordingly, he warned merchants to keep a reserve for emergencies and to avoid the temptation of sinking all their credit into financial and trading ventures on the seas and abroad: "he who is furthest from his goods is nearest to his loss." [15] Assets might well outweigh liabilities; even so, the problem was to secure a desirable liquidity for immediate needs. Failed merchants might have survived, "but that being out of their monies, and their monies out of the kingdom, maketh them to go out of their credits." [16] Distant though the wealth might be, the commercial man was tied to it not as master but as slave. The least rumor was enough to galvanize creditors. Malynes, who loved proverbs and homilies, recalled the ape tied to a clog who thought he kept it though it kept him.[17]

Certainly there were many commercial disasters, and it has to be remembered that laws and procedures concerning debt, irrespective of the bankruptcy statutes, were also capable of destroying a merchant whose credit should have been good. It has been suggested that for the seventeenth century as a whole the rate of business failure was high. The long-term rate of return on trading capital was low. In particular, much capital invested before the Civil War in discovery, colonies, and the development of heavy industry "sank without trace." [18]

Merchants had to exist amid circumstances which rarely promised consistent good fortune. "A man might make one hundred per cent profit, followed by one hundred per cent loss, in the same business within a year." [19] The ablest merchant could be shattered by bad luck, and many were more deficient than able in their accounting methods and business techniques. In any case, the only real guarantee against disaster was to keep disproportionately large sums in safe reserve. This meant that the return of profit would be small, but in building up capital, careful saving was more important than quick earnings.[20] Malynes would have agreed. As it was, too many did not have such reserves or, possibly through no fault of their own, found that too much money had been committed unfortunately. "Though interest at the statutory rate was charged for forbearance, large sums were lost or tied up in doubtful and desperate debts and unpaid bills; often men with limited capital could not wait for good market conditions and were forced to sell at a loss." [21]

Survival in this climate was not an easy matter. Concentration upon secure trades, albeit accepting a low return, might seem to have been the sensible policy. Perhaps all trades were insecure, and the element of risk may have been greater than the average returns received by the poorer merchants.[22] Furthermore, some people entangled themselves in situations which were hopeless by any standard. A classic Elizabethan example is provided by Michael Lok, whose association with Frobisher in the Cathay Company became a mining speculation carried on with a "reckless improvidence . . . well-nigh incredible to modern minds." In fairness to Coke, Stone, and others, it was also incredible to some contemporaries. Lok, who had committed his entire fortune and credit, was destroyed by his associates and called to account by all the creditors. He was incarcerated in a debtor's prison, and even Frobisher assailed him. "Undoubtedly he was to blame, but for folly and not fraud." [23]

A marine or other disaster could occasion widespread failures as overextended merchants struggled to meet obligations which would not otherwise have worried them, and which might not have been cata-

---

[14] Supple, p. 174. L. Stone, *An Elizabethan: Sir Horatio Palavacino* (Oxford, 1956), pp. 225–228.

[15] Malynes, *Lex Mercatoria*, p. 156.

[16] G. de Malynes, *The Maintenance of Free Trade* (London, 1622), p. 123.

[17] Malynes, *Lex Mercatoria*, p. 156.

[18] Grassby, "The Rate of Profit," p. 732. R. Grassby, "The Personal Wealth of the Business Community in Seventeenth-Century England," *Ec.HR*, 2nd ser. (1970) **22**: p. 223. An outstanding example is provided by the spectacular failure of the Courteens, which drained and shattered the wealth of their relative by marriage, John, first earl of Bridgewater, the son of Lord Chancellor Ellesmere.

[19] Grassby, "The Rate of Profit," p. 738.

[20] *Ibid.*

[21] *Ibid.*, p. 737.

[22] *Ibid.*, p. 733.

[23] J. A. Williamson, *The Age of Drake* (London, 1960), pp. 153–165. See Carole Shammas, "The 'Invisible Merchant' and Property Rights," *Business History* 17 (1975): pp. 95–108.

strophic if they had been given further time.[24] From this point of view, it was difficult to accept the realities of the situation as created by statute. Merchants could appreciate that failure was a misfortune for both creditors and debtors, but some suspected that the specification of behavior which constituted an act of bankruptcy had very little to do with mercantile practice. It was an artificial creation of legislation cast into the deep seas of preexisting law, the product of a social system which strove to establish clear-cut rules towards stability. Furthermore, the lawyers, legislators, and judges who had assumed the responsibility for defining bankruptcy were inclined to think in terms of fraudulent behavior. While not discounting underhand dealings and the regular element of risk in business, the merchant still had to accept that the status of being a bankrupt was determined by an arbitrary legal rule. It was not unlike driving on the wrong side of the road. This was really the point made by Malynes. The laws were there. If they were not enforced there would be chaos, and merchants who failed to make their dispositions with an eye to these laws were foolish.

The establishment of a set of rules which were theoretical, rather than hewed out of the needs and experience of commerce, made it possible to suppose that the only determining factor was chance. If Malynes was not really hostile to the bankruptcy statutes, he nonetheless noted their divorce from trading practice. Others used similar conclusions to buttress their dislike of the law as it stood, or to fuel arguments about advantages which change might bring for the economy and thus for the nation.

Honesty and dishonesty, despite lawyers who harped on fraud, had indeed ceased to count when chance and circumstance brought some within one sphere of technicality whereas it allowed or compelled others to stay outside. Many merchants and even some great clothiers could withstand the strain put upon them in times of general commercial difficulty,[25] but this was not always what mattered. Theoretically a merchant or trader, who was quite capable of keeping his head above water, might do something which would put him within the scope of the statutes and so encourage his creditors to petition for a commission. This rarely happened to the great ones, but the possibility was annoying. Bankruptcy had little to do with financial inability—although this might fairly be deduced from behavior—because it was anchored to a list of actions mentioned in legislation, actions which often needed interpretation. As Professor Harper has written of the navigation acts: "the work of Parliament was done, but the acts on the statute books were not the law applied at the waterside." [26]

Merchants were disgruntled. Acid comments were made in the Restoration period when economic optimism encouraged inquiries into the means whereby England's prosperity could be developed. Capital for investment might come from surplus agricultural production, re-exports, or foreign trade. There seemed some reason to query devices which strained credit.[27] Whether or not any particular year seemed good or bad, questions were naturally raised. The Lords committee on the decay of rents and trade was told in 1669 that the statutes of artificers and bankrupts were prejudicial to trade. In 1674, Sir Richard Haines painted a gloomy picture: "a general poverty seems to have invaded the whole nation, leases being continually thrown up in the country, and tradesmen daily breaking in the City." Not so long after, it was asked why traders "were never so poor or broke so fast (thought never so fine) as now." [28]

It is difficult to measure such things, but there seems very little reason to believe that bankruptcy laws actually damaged trade. Their greatest impact was on the habits of traders. The divergence between commercial and legal priorities should not be exaggerated or used to draw stark conclusions in the wrong direction. As a nineteenth-century observer remarked, there was bound to be a relationship if only because social problems were tackled in the courts and by legislation, but this was not a one-way relationship. In the end, legal rules had to be accommodated to social habits. Perhaps, as Welbourne has concluded for the Hanoverian period, it was the machinery of administration rather than the bankruptcy law itself which justified disquiet. Whatever may be said of lawyers and the stupidity and delays of law, "perhaps the pathology of the business world deserves a little closer attention than it has received from students of risk." [29]

Malynes had concentrated upon merchants trading overseas. Even so his adversary, Misselden, felt that they were underestimated, not to say besmirched, by Malynes, whose knowledge, logic, and personal career offended him. He "is not of us." Readers were warned against those who came in sheep's clothing,

[24] See N. S. B. Gras, *Business and Capitalism* (New York, 1939), p. 161.

[25] Supple, p. 11.

[26] L. A. Harper, *The English Navigation Laws* (New York, 1939), p. 63.

[27] See K. G. Davies, "Joint-Stock Investment in the Later Seventeenth Century," *Essays in Economic History*, ed. E. M. Carus-Wilson 2 (London, 1962): p. 275.

[28] *Seventeenth-Century Economic Documents*, pp. 70, 88. (Sir William Petyt), "*Britania Languens* or A Discourse of Trade" (1680), *Early English Tracts on Commerce*, ed. J. R. McCulloch. (Cambridge, 1952), p. 455. It has been suggested that tradesmen extended credit because they had little choice. Stone, *Aristocracy*, p. 515. Bankruptcy laws can, perhaps, be viewed in part as an undeserved penalty of this compulsion.

[29] *Suggestions* (?1819), f. 2. Welbourne, pp. 51, 62.

though Malynes was "so easy a combatant, that a man may give him any advantage of the weapon." It was, in truth, a debate marked by animosity. "I marvel who made Malynes a law-maker for merchants, if he be so ignorant of their profession! . . . The profession of a merchant is more noble than to be so disabled and disgraced by such a fellow as Malynes is." [30]

Misselden was not concerned with bankruptcy as such, but like many contemporaries he was appalled by the nature and prolixity of legal proceedings. He contrasted deficient (lack of money, for example) with efficient causes of the decay of trade. Among the latter, usury and unnecessary suits in law occupied a high place. The situation would be vastly improved if only "men bestowed half that study and cost in trade, which nowadays is spent in temerous and rash suits of law. . . ." He harshly criticized the development of fictions and their attendant personnel—those wretched fellows, John Doe and Richard Roe, and those dubious sureties, John Cheape and Richard Side.[31] The total picture was depressing. "A great number of his Majesty's good and loving subjects are vexed, imprisoned, impoverished, and overthrown. And while the litigants strive together, another taketh away the fish . . . and the men's time and means being spent in law which should be employed in trade. . . ." Again and again the point was hammered home: "no kingdom hath better laws; no kingdom so full fraught with tedious, needless, endless suits of law." He suggested that some practices in restraint of litigation employed at Lyons, Rouen, and Toulouse might be adapted with benefit to English conditions. There was, however, a gleam of hope: "suits of law do seem immortal, time doth increase them and length of time would not determine them, if the wisdom of those great fathers of the law did not put an end to the malice of litigants, as is now worthily observed in Chancery, to his honor and memory that hath so happily begun the same." [32] He added the suggestion that ordinary courts could be relieved by having mercantile cases diverted to authorized experts. Parliament could do something to improve the situation, and he instanced with approval the system of marine insurance founded by statute in 1601.[33]

In deploring the legal position, Misselden reproved merchants who seemed incapable of avoiding litigation. The commercial man might think that his class wished to avoid unnecessary dealings with the alien breed of lawyers, but this was little more than part of a tendency to keep close to their own mercantile society. It was merchants and traders themselves who chose to use, or not to use, the rules provided by the legal system. They were the sponsors of litigation. Anyone who has made a study of the legal records will appreciate the force of Professor Willan's remark that "merchants defended their rights, or alleged rights, to personal property with the same tenacity as Elizabethan landowners defended their titles, or alleged titles, to real property." [34] Whatever the pressures imposed upon them, merchants and traders were likely to be the creditors who decided to petition for a commission of bankruptcy.

In a situation recalling the pot that termed the kettle black, standard complaints against the law and the legal profession were intensified. Lawyers and procedures, it was later asserted, combined to produce inappropriate, long-winded, and costly requirements which were damaging to trade.[35] It was particularly resented that the harm done to others should be rewarded with material success, something that was probably overestimated. Early in the reign of Charles I, a bank was proposed to finance war expenditures and otherwise make loans at five per cent. It was to be funded in part by an annual levy on attorneys, clerks, and lawyers since these, it was argued, were seldom or never taxed in respect of military service or required to serve in person. Instead they lived "safe and secure" while attending their "benefits and profits." [36]

It was for their easy condemnation of lawyers and gentlemen that Thomas Mun chided his fellow merchants. He had written a paper at the behest of the East India Company and thus of the elite in overseas commerce and their landed associates and investors. This tract, which was praised by Misselden,[37] was expanded into a larger work. Even if lawyers were covetous, Mun argued, there could be little ill effect without the perverse nature of litigants. Merchants chose to go to law, and doubtless some lost their money through the exercise of this choice. The legal profession, which he described as "noble," was a necessity even if the actual cases, delays and charges could be represented as destructive of individuals and their estates. He could not see that this had any real impact on the economic position of the country. Furthermore, he was inclined to reject most of the criticism directed against the nobility, the gentry, and

[30] E. Misselden, *The Circle of Commerce* (London, 1623), preface and pp. 17–19, 111. Malynes was swift to counterattack against Misselden's arguments and "uncivil speeches." *The Center of the Circle of Commerce* (London, 1623).

[31] These developments were often obstructive, but in other areas fictions were ways in which courts tried to innovate and keep in touch with changing demands.

[32] This seems to refer to Bacon, but the wording is ambiguous.

[33] E. Misselden, *Free Trade, or the Meanes to Make Trade Florish* (London, 1622), pp. 29, 32, 33–34, 119, 120, 122–123.

[34] T. S. Willan, *Studies in Elizabethan Foreign Trade* (Manchester, 1959), p. 131.

[35] (Petyt), "*Britania Languens*," pp. 368, 378–379.

[36] Richards, pp. 94–95.

[37] Misselden, *Circle of Commerce*.

others because of their presumed overspending on buildings, fine clothes, and other luxuries.[38]

Although comment can at times be found, it is only with Defoe, who was personally involved, that there emerges a major critic of the bankruptcy laws who was more concerned with tradesmen than with international merchants. Like Dekker, who was also very much aware of the distinction, Defoe could be extravagant and imaginative in his descriptions and conclusions, but one can only agree with his opinion, published in 1697, that the current situation was absurd. The 1624 statute might well have been justified by circumstances at the time, but decades had passed and conditions were now vastly different. Society and law, business and legal procedures, had changed. Debtors had once again developed too many means of frustrating or evading the statutes. Others, who could not escape, were trapped. These were treated with an insane cruelty which did not benefit the creditor save to satisfy his malice.[39]

Defoe, who had his own axes to grind, succeeded across thirty years in castigating all elements involved in bankruptcy. According to him, the law was generally good, but in this instance it was hopeless. Commissions were incompetent, consuming money that might otherwise have been used for payment of debts. Any sensible creditor would arrange a composition according to the understood practices of the business community; those that opted for statutory procedures were stupid or vile. Traders were worthy, but too many drifted into disaster through luxurious living, enjoyable pastimes, early marriages, and inept business methods, particularly in the giving and taking of credit. Some bankrupts were unfortunates, but it was Defoe's opinion that most of them deserved to be called knaves and dishonest men. Yet whatever might be thought of bankrupts, nothing could justify the statutes which Defoe described as barbarous. "It leaves the debtor no way to show himself honest . . . for it makes him perfectly uncapable of any thing but *starving.*" This ghastly legislation, which flouted the commercial instinct to secure compositions, "for ever shuts up all doors to the debtor's recovery; as if breaking were a crime so capital, that he ought to be cast out of human society, and exposed to extremeties worse than death."[40]

Adam Smith, not very concerned with the inadequate shackles of legal rules, wrote comments not unlike those of Malynes. Failure (and possibly bankruptcy) was implicit in the very nature of trade: it occurred most frequently in hazardous trades. In this respect, Smith's writings reflect an air of resignation as to the facts of life.[41] A greater change of emphasis is to be seen in the writings of a lawyer. Blackstone, who was as ready to condemn extravagant living as Coke had been, classified bankruptcy as the eighth way in English law whereby lands and tenements might be forfeited.[42] It might even be seen as a commendable assistance to commerce. This appraisal might be different from that of Coke, but Blackstone too could be confident in the virtues of his law; and it must be remembered that statutory amendments of the eighteenth century had introduced a variety of changes, notably the discharge, which had considerable significance.[43]

Blackstone admired English law, but many popular voices conceived bankruptcy as a fraud. Oliver Goldsmith had previously expressed current doubts about commercial wealth.[44] Bankruptcy, wrote a pamphleteer, "is now considered an infallible method for one in tattered circumstances to make himself whole again. It is called the emetic of an undone man." A picture of deceit was painted. "One auspicious morning" a man, at the height of his financial reputation, puts his most valuable effects into a casket and steals away. Those who have loaned him money panic and offer a two-thirds composition, but receive no answer. "The creditors meet; they come, they go; they torment themselves." Eventually they "whisper" that they are willing to *lose* two-thirds. Everything is arranged, and the bankrupt reappears with some thousands in specie. "Will not a man who takes such prudential steps but once in his life be able to make a figure ever after?"[45]

Popular opinion would never take kindly to the bankrupt. The shades of uncertainty were expressed in an American book review, written in 1834.

> But it is sometimes said that most debtors, who do not pay their debts, are in some degree guilty, and merit punishment. This seems to us not quite true. Some debtors, we admit, are mere swindlers and sharpers. Others have become involved by daring speculations. Some are the victims of extravagance. Others fail from

[38] L. Muchmore, "A Note on Thomas Mun's 'England's Treasure by Forraign Trade'," *Ec.HR*, 2nd ser. **23** (1970): pp. 498–503. T. Mun, *England's Treasure by Forraign Trade*, ed. of 1664 (Oxford, 1959), pp. 59–60.

[39] Defoe, *Essay Upon Projects*, pp. 195–196.

[40] *Ibid.*, pp. 191, 194. D. Defoe, *The Complete English Tradesman* **1** (London, 1726): pp. 95–96 *et passim*. See also D. Defoe, *Remarks on the Bill to Prevent Frauds Committed by Bankrupts* (London, 1706).

[41] Adam Smith, pp. 111, 325.

[42] The other seven were: by crimes and misdemeanors; by alienation contrary to law; by non-presentation, when the forfeiture was deemed to be a lapse; by simony; by non-performance of conditions; by waste; by breach of copyhold customs. Blackstone **2**: pp. 267, 284.

[43] Blackstone, who was certainly eager to applaud restraints upon mercantile excess, could refer, somewhat in the manner of Smith, to the bankrupt as an "unfortunate person," but the adjective was more redolent of meaning than it sometimes is today. *Ibid.* **2**: p. 284.

[44] Wilson, p. 12. See also M. M. Goldsmith, "Mandeville and the Spirit of Capitalism," *The Journal of British Studies* **17** (1977): pp. 63–81.

[45] *The Bankrupt: A Modern Character* (n.d.).

want of skill and judgment in conducting their business. We find in the conduct of debtors every moral shade, from gross fraud to the slightest negligence and entire innocence. The high degrees of fraud are comparatively rare. Slighter degrees of misconduct are more common. But judged by the current rules of mercantile honesty, we believe the majority of insolvent debtors upright and honorable.[46]

The anonymous writer was rather smug, but the points considered could have been applied to the Elizabethan and early Stuart period. Notions of property might shift, but they did not differ to a very great degree when it came to an interpretation of individual action. Elizabethans believed in land, and nineteenth-century Bostonians believed in wealth. The man who failed to live up to these assumptions, whether by accident or design, had offended against society.

English law, by the very nature of its medieval legacy, distinguished to some extent between commercial wealth and landed property. It reflected the attitudes of those who stayed in one place and in one social position. It had difficulty in adapting to a social mobility which was natural. The land was the life of the law and, wrote Plucknett, "the separation of commerce from the normal occupation of the nation was further emphasized by the fact that the merchants had their own organization and their own law." Only as late as 1690 did the law embrace the possibility that one who was not a merchant might be party to a bill of exchange.[47] This does not mean that landed men were not vitally interested in commerce. Agriculture, the source of income or employment for most people, was "itself increasingly marked by the application of capital, enterprise, novel methods, and the quest for markets. The dynamic of the time was commercial." [48] Furthermore, non-merchant participation along the lines of investment was increasingly important. Merchants, for their part, became landowners, and the two groups intermarried. One has only to look at the career of Cranfield or the disastrous association of the Earl of Bridgewater with the Courteens. Professor Stone's study of Palaviacino provides "an almost perfect textbook case of this transformation of merchant into landowner. . . ." [49] English social life was fluid. It was possible to move from one level to another. That hybrid, the merchant-landowning-gentleman, however, is hardly visible. While landed families fueled business ranks, and others managed to obscure their mercantile origins, there was always something which distinguished the merchant from the rest of society. "What was peculiar to the merchant was the form in which his wealth was held and the use which he made of his assets." [50]

Apart from the clarification provided by the act of 1662, there was no legislation for seven decades after 1624. Throughout this time, social distinctions were hardened and perpetuated. The point was doubtless appreciated by Defoe.[51] There were two basic assumptions enshrined in the statutes of 1571, 1604, and 1624. In the first place, it was supposed that merchants and traders, that is, international merchants, great financiers, shopkeepers, and craftsmen, could be lumped together in a single category. Secondly, it was assumed that in this context all traders, merchants and retailers, could be separated rationally from landed gentlemen. If the latter notion caused some trouble, as it was also to do in the eighteenth century, it was the first supposition which was most strikingly out of touch with the conventions of the business world.

Economic historians have long recognized that English conditions separated the merchant, in the sense of being an exporter or importer, from the trader.[52] Malynes, Misselden, and Mun wrote from the viewpoint of their own kind. This is understandable, and people associated with that circle were possibly more literate and sophisticated than the average run of retailers, but it means that we cannot take them as representing the views of traders and shopkeepers. There was a gulf between the two groups. Indeed the distinction between foreign trade and retail trading or shopkeeping was long established in many organizations before it was reflected, for example, in the 1605 charter of the Levant Company and the 1611 charter of the French merchants. Just as the Inns of Court strengthened their barriers against attorneys, so the great merchants wished to have little to do with tradesmen and others on whom they looked down. For a member of one of these companies to be a retailer, remarked Heckscher, was as much a crime as "offenses and the practices of evil demeanor." [53]

Distinctions within the business community were complex and not easy for some contemporaries to grasp. Generally, it was conventional to rely on three main categories: merchants (overseas traders);

[46] From *American Jurist* 11 (1834): cited Costigan, p. 107, n. 15.

[47] Plucknett, pp. 65–66.

[48] Wilson, p. x.

[49] Stone, *Palaviacino*, p. 268.

[50] R. Grassby, "English Merchant Capitalism in the late Seventeenth Century. The Composition of Business Fortunes," *Past and Present* 46 (Feb. 1970): pp. 87–88.

[51] See above, p. 57.

[52] Sutherland, p. 156.

[53] E. F. Heckscher, *Mercantilism*, rev. ed. E. F. Söderlund, 1 (London, 1955): pp. 378–379. Shopkeepers and retailers were excluded from the Spanish Company. Pauline Croft, *The Spanish Company*, London Rec. Soc. (London, 1973), p. xxxv. For the fifteenth-century position, including gradations of prejudice towards retail trade among the gentry, see Sylvia L. Thrupp, *The Merchant Class of Medieval London* (Chicago, 1948), chap. 6, "Trade and Gentility."

tradesmen (skilled craftsmen); and retailers (those who sold the goods of others).[54] Defoe, however, said that *tradesman* meant different things in different parts of the British Isles, but that in England generally it meant wholesalers or retailers "who do not actually work upon, make, or manufacture the goods they sell." He would not apply the word *tradesman* to those who engaged in handicrafts and manufactures. He was, however, talking about two groups who occupied the middle ground: below them he placed workmen, laborers, and servants; above he placed merchants and explained that in England this word involved foreign commerce.[55]

In lumping together all who made their living through merchandise and trade, the bankruptcy statutes glossed over vast social distinctions which were very real. In the same breath, the statutes also created a legal fence between the upper echelons of commerce and landed gentlemen. This too was not always in accordance with the facts of either society or the law in general. Edward Chamberlayne pointed out that merchants trading abroad had a reputation which far exceeded that of chapmen or others who lived by buying and selling. These latter were a "baser sort of people" whereas "to become a merchant of foreign commerce, without serving any apprenticeship, hath been allowed no disparagement to a gentleman born, especially to a younger brother." [56] Indeed, he wrote, "in cases and causes, the law of England hath conceived a better opinion of the yeomanry that occupy lands, than of tradesmen, artificers or laborers." [57]

Contemporaries were by no means entirely clear about their own society and its distinctions. Historians of our own day, not to mention those of the past, have engaged in rewarding studies of social evolution, class, and occupational distinction. Clear guidelines, however, cannot be drawn. Statutes must be appreciated in terms of the social assumptions at the time of their enactment. With respect to subsequent interpretation before the courts, similar considerations must be kept constantly in mind. There can be no subject which more demands an awareness of such themes, even though conclusions are impossible, than bankruptcy. We may not be able to describe how men in Parliament thought, but at least the question can be asked and kept to the fore. If we are right in supposing that the statutes fluffed the realities of contemporary social distinction, may it not be supposed that a clue can be found in the composition of Parliament?

In the eighteenth century the discharge was introduced; in the next some significant changes were made in the classification of those who could become bankrupt. It was a slow process, but it is one matched by the growing importance in politics and society of merchants, financiers, and industrialists. Their presence was evident in the House of Commons, it was not absent from the House of Lords, and increasingly they gained the ear of government. This was not true of those Tudor and Jacobean parliaments which engineered and passed the initial banruptcy statutes.

The Henrician statute, whatever its imperfections of language, was passed at a time when fifteenth-century rules governing the qualifications of a member of Parliament were still accorded some respect. The decisive period, that between 1571 and 1624, represents those years in which gentlemen flooded the House of Commons through their ability to secure election in the boroughs. During the parliaments of Elizabeth, James I, and Charles I, men of business were a distinct minority in the House of Commons. One analysis suggests that there were only forty-two commercial men ("merchants") among the 464 members of Parliament who sat in 1614.[58] It is not impossible that delusions about maritime warfare and its profits may have been engendered by the small number of merchants who actually sat in the House of Commons.[59] It is, of course, true that London financiers might on occasion exercise a dramatic authority. This was most apparent early in 1641 when money had to be raised to satisfy the Scots and calm a disorderly rabble of defeated English soldiers. Situations such as this were rare, and an analysis of the Commons which met in November, 1640, indicates the dominant strength of landed interests.[60]

---

[54] Grassby, "Personal Wealth," pp. 222–223.

[55] Defoe, *Complete Tradesman* 1: pp. 1–3. There was no real definition of a trader at law; or rather there were different strands of development for the interpretation of different statutes.

[56] Chamberlayne, *State of England*, pp. 444–445. He was pointing out that by law a ward within age could bring an action for disparagement against his guardian for offering marriage with a tradesman or chapman. There are examples of men engaged in mundane occupations being able to bear the style of gentleman. Wilson, p. 14. This may give force to a conclusion that for the purposes of the House of Commons during the early Long Parliament "a merchant was probably anyone who so regarded himself." D. Brunton and D. H. Pennington, *Members of the Long Parliament* (London, 1954), p. 53. Chap. 4 of this book is valuable. I do not, however, think that the impression of an almost casual approach towards social distinctions should be taken very far. The House of Commons was a community in itself, that was its secret, but it was not English society.

[57] Chamberlayne, p. 442.

[58] T. L. Moir, *The Addled Parliament of 1614* (Oxford, 1958), p. 57.

[59] J. P. Kenyon, *The Stuart Constitution* (Cambridge, 1966), p. 29.

[60] A breakdown of the occupations and family status of members called to the Long Parliament suggests that there were fifty-five merchants and tradesmen out of a total of 547. Of the "tradesmen"—this classification ignores a very necessary distinction—two were elder sons of "knights and gentlemen," four were younger sons, three were sons of "new gentry," one was the son of a churchman, and another was the son of a

If men of commerce were a weak force in Elizabethan and early Stuart parliaments, retailers and craftsmen counted for nothing. The attitude of authority has been delicately described by Professor Wilson.

> Whether "government" meant Privy Council under the monarchy or the Council of State in Commonwealth times, it listened to merchant petitions, sometimes accepting, sometimes rejecting. It was rarely dictated to, even though the early Stuarts often stooped to folly. On the rare occasions when Government gave in to the clamor of the City—as it did over the second Dutch War—it was persuaded less by the merchants themselves than by a court clique who thought they could further their own interests by an alliance with the City.[61]

Since the essence of policy was paternal, there was care for trade but not for traders. It has been observed that "a bankrupt merchant left the state unmoved, but a ship rotting by the quayside was a matter for concern." [62] The emphasis on landed property increased. By a statute of 1711, impressive landed qualifications were expected of members of Parliament.[63] It became necessary to be a freeholder, even to be a juryman: "full citizenship, in fact, was open only to the property holder," [64] and for "property," read "land." Professor Wilson's conclusions carry an unmistakable ring of truth.

> The suspicion of business wealth as a social solvent and a certain lingering nostalgia for an ordered, traditional society was to die hard. . . . Few successful businessmen passed immediately into the charmed circle of government, and the few who did—like Cranfield—had to face powerful opposition from the older incumbents of office who regarded them as upstarts. Adam Smith's picture of seventeenth-century governments as puppets of a cunning clique of merchants was a long way wide of the mark.[65]

Although there were to be many significant developments affecting commerce in the seventeenth century, landed producers were more successful than merchants in attaining a revaluation of legal rules and limitations. Business wealth was small in comparison with "the capital assets of the Crown, the Church, and the landed interest." The merchants, it has been observed, "were outnumbered, divided, and socially disoriented," and "trade could hardly have been a wide channel of social and economic advancement." [66] Certainly, they lacked effective political power, and they could have had little influence on the framing of the early bankruptcy statutes. Retailers and shopkeepers were even less influential, and their voices were not heard in Parliament. For all the participation of commercial members of Parliament—those for London, Newcastle, and York were specifically mentioned in 1604—Commons committees working on bankruptcy bills represent the usual dominance of landed gentry and lawyers.[67]

If we turn to the eighteenth century and the Regency period, gentlemen and peers who felt insulted when called upon to meet a tradesman's bill are a recognizable element. A shopkeeper who adopted similar standards would meet with short shrift, even though he might have run into difficulty through allowing credit to his gentry customers. These were common attitudes which Hanoverians had inherited. A statute of 1610 placed considerable onus on tradesmen by discharging all debts claimed from customers after twelve months if based upon shop books or accounts. Quite rightly intended to prevent double payments, it pointed out that buyers could not be expected to keep receipts for so long a period. Instead, before expiry of the allowed time, the shopkeeper was told that he ought to obtain bills or obligations acknowledging the sum due or commence action at law. This requirement, it was stressed with rare regard for these particular distinctions, did not apply to the commercial transactions of "merchant and merchant, merchant and tradesman, or between tradesman and tradesman." According to a treatise subtitled "The Tickling Torture" the courtier neither could nor wanted to pay, the country gentleman preferred that his sureties should pay, and the "citizen" was pleased to pay according to some rate which might amount to no more than five shillings in the pound.[68]

We have heard about the difficulties of the aristocracy, for whom the Elizabethan and early Stuart period has been represented as involving a crisis of confidence, and about the misfortunes of at least one section of the gentry. Aristocracy and gentry may represent little more than devious footnotes of social classification, but the agonies and ambitions, legal or economic, of social mobility represent real and compelling themes. We are aware of contemporary fears of vagabondage and thus of a hunger march of peasants driven off the land. These fears were exaggerated, but there was at one time a flow of population,

---

lawyer. Twenty-seven came from trading families, three were sons of yeomen, and one was the son of a mariner. The social origins of the remainder could not be determined. Gentlemen (333) comprised the largest group. There were seventy-four "lawyers," twenty-seven royal officials, and twenty-two courtiers. Mary F. Keeler, *The Long Parliament 1640–1641. A Biographical Study of its Members*, Mem. Amer. Philos. Soc. **36** (Philadelphia, 1954): pp. 21, n. 108, 23 (Table 5).

[61] Wilson, pp. 12–13.

[62] R. W. K. Hinton, "The Mercantile System in the Time of Thomas Mun," *Ec.HR*, 2nd ser. **8** (1955): p. 279.

[63] 9 Anne c. 5.

[64] Wilson, p. 9.

[65] *Ibid.*, pp. 12–13. See also C. Wilson, "Government Policy and Private Interest in Modern English History," *Historical Studies*, ed. T. W. Moody **6** (London, 1968): pp. 85–99.

[66] Grassby, "English Merchant Capitalism," p. 87; "The Rate of Profit," p. 733.

[67] *CJ* 1: pp. 208–209, 228, 552.

[68] 7 James I c. 10. Powel, *The Mysterie of Lending and Borrowing*, pp. 13, 18.

not least from decaying towns, towards London. It is reasonable to note the growing dominance of the metropolis, and the erratic fortunes of other ports. Clerks and officials in the institutions of Westminster felt threatened by patentees, subordinates, and public criticism. It would seem that many sections of the community were afflicted, but what are we to make of tradesmen and merchants?

Some merchants and traders were rich, and others were poor; some fell and others rose. These fluctuations in society were irrelevant. The bankruptcy statutes had ensured that a man who lived through merchandise was possibly circumscribed by a law which did not cover those who relied upon estates, cash crops, and investment.

While clear definition of social groupings is both difficult and dangerous, Sir Lewis Namier recognized the necessity of distinctions as it affected the membership of the House of Commons. "Merchants in the eighteenth century meant businessmen, and the term was as wide as trade is even now; bankers and manufacturers were included. But I do not include among the merchants country gentlemen who owned mines or even iron works but clearly did not belong to the business community . . . ." [69] For an earlier period, that after 1688, Professor Plumb has referred to a confirmation of the authority of certain men of property "whose tap-root was in land but whose side-roots reached out to commerce, industry, and finance." [70] The description is valuable. For while the bankruptcy statutes implied an existing social distinction, drew the lines of that distinction yet more firmly, and helped to maintain it, it still does not follow that the distinction was a practical one. Law is often seen as a reflection of society, and this is true of the early bankruptcy statutes and the decisions made upon them in the early seventeenth century. Nonetheless the lawmakers, both legislators and judges, while they did their best to handle immediate problems, rather dodged the questions posed by those "side-roots." The law of bankruptcy was not particularly suited to the problems of merchants, as distinguished from the shopkeepers and small manufacturers such as bakers and shoemakers.

John Wheeler, writing late in Elizabeth's reign, protested against those who

> scorn to be called merchants. Whereas indeed merchandise, which is used by way of proper vocation, being rightly considered of, is not to be despised, or accounted base by men of judgement, but to the contrary . . . the estate is honorable, and may be exercised not only of those of the third estate (as we term them) but also by the nobles, and chiefest men of this realm with commendable profit, and without any derogation to their nobilities, high degrees and conditions. . . . [71]

But it was not to be. "Distrust of the self-made man of money, and an instinctive belief in government by traditional means and a traditional ruling class was strong in the seventeenth century." [72] Not without reason did Jenks describe the Tudor and Stuart bankruptcy statutes as representing "pitiless severity . . . towards the unfortunate merchant." [73] This is a distortion only in its concentration upon the word *merchant* rather than upon shopkeepers and tradesmen. The power of commerce would grow, but this cannot easily be equated with the social or political status accorded to merchants and traders.

Professor Plumb has argued that after 1688 the "middle class" thrived socially and economically, but not politically. The phrase "middle class" is of dubious value for this period and, in any case, it has broader connotations than *trader* or similar terms. However, his exposition of this argument is to the point. "The power of the land and of commerce fused to create a paradise for gentlemen, for the aristocracy of birth; it thus became much easier for England to adopt an imperial authority . . . rather than to adjust its institutions and its social system to the needs of an industrial society." [74] Even in the late nineteenth century, there could still be a feeling that the man who was "in trade" was "not quite, quite." Bagehot gave his impression of this attitude. "The order of nobility is of great use, too, not only in what it creates but in what it prevents. It prevents the rule of wealth—the religion of gold. This is the obvious and natural idol of the Anglo-Saxon. He is always trying to make money; he reckons everything in coin; he bows down before a great heap, and gallops as he passes a little heap." [75]

Tudor and early Stuart bankruptcy statutes had been framed by men who assumed social distinctions which were not so very diverse from Victorian attitudes. Yet the nature of debt and credit is practical: it is a matter of what men do and not of how they appear to others; even though this always plays a part in any decision to extend credit.

---

[69] Namier, p. 49, n. 1.

[70] J. H. Plumb, *The Growth of Political Stability in England, 1675–1725* (London, 1967), p. 69.

[71] J. Wheeler, *A Treatise of Commerce* (1601), ed. G. B. Hotchkiss (New York, 1931), p. 7. Note the discussion provided by Stone, *Aristocracy*, pp. 335 *et seq.*

[72] Wilson, p. 12.

[73] Jenks, p. 383.

[74] Plumb, p. 187.

[75] W. Bagehot, *The English Constitution* (1933), p. 80, cited Wilson, p. 12.

INDEX

www.ingramcontent.com/pod-product-compliance
Lightning Source LLC
LaVergne TN
LVHW061730220926
848484LV00026B/2447
* 9 7 8 1 4 2 2 3 7 4 9 5 5 *